Cybersecurity Threat Hunting for Beginners

Proactively Detect and Mitigate Cybersecurity Threats

Greyson Chesterfield

COPYRIGHT

DISCLAIMER

The information provided in this book is for general informational purposes only. All content in this book reflects the author's views and is based on their research, knowledge, and experiences. The author and publisher make no representations or warranties of any kind concerning the completeness, accuracy, reliability, suitability, or availability of the information contained herein.

This book is not intended to be a substitute for professional advice, diagnosis, or treatment. Readers should seek professional advice for any specific concerns or conditions. The author and publisher disclaim any liability or responsibility for any direct, indirect, incidental, or consequential loss or damage arising from the use of the information contained in this book.

Contents

Introduction: The Need for Threat Hunting

What is Cybersecurity Threat Hunting?

Definition of Threat Hunting and Why It's Essential

Cybersecurity **threat hunting** refers to the proactive process of searching for signs of malicious activities or cyber threats within an organization's network. Unlike traditional cybersecurity measures, which are designed to detect known threats based on predefined patterns or signatures, threat hunting goes a step further. It involves actively searching for indicators of compromise (IOCs) or unusual patterns of behavior that could signal a potential threat, even if those threats haven't been detected by automated systems.

Threat hunting is essential because cyber threats are continuously evolving, and the complexity of modern attacks is often beyond the detection capabilities of conventional security systems. Relying solely on reactive measures such as firewalls, antivirus software, or intrusion detection systems (IDS) may not be sufficient to protect against more sophisticated or novel attacks.

In threat hunting, cybersecurity professionals do not wait for alarms to go off. Instead, they search for clues or signs of activity that indicate an adversary might have already infiltrated the system or is attempting to do so.

How Threat Hunting Differs from Traditional Security Measures (Reactive vs. Proactive)

Traditional cybersecurity relies heavily on **reactive** measures such as firewalls, antivirus, and intrusion prevention systems (IPS) to prevent attacks. These tools are designed to detect and block known threats based on pre-configured rules or signatures. When an attack occurs, the system reacts by either blocking the malicious activity or alerting security teams. While these measures are important, they have limitations.

For example, they can't detect **zero-day vulnerabilities** (new, previously unknown threats) or attacks that have been specifically crafted to evade signature-based detection. They are also reactive, meaning that they only respond after the attack has occurred or been detected by other means.

In contrast, **threat hunting** is a **proactive** approach. It seeks to identify threats before they cause damage by actively searching for patterns, anomalies, and unusual behavior. This method allows organizations to detect and mitigate threats early in their lifecycle, sometimes even before they fully execute their malicious actions. Essentially, threat hunters are always on the lookout for potential threats, not just responding to alerts after they happen.

Real-World Example: Case of a Data Breach that Could Have Been Avoided with Proactive Threat Hunting

A well-known example of how proactive threat hunting could have prevented a major data breach is the **Target data breach** of 2013. Hackers gained access to Target's internal network via stolen credentials from a third-party vendor. Once inside, they moved laterally across the network and accessed sensitive customer data, including credit card information.

While traditional security measures, like firewalls and antivirus, were in place, the attack went undetected for several weeks. This was partly because the organization lacked a proactive threat-hunting program that could have identified suspicious activity during the early stages of the attack. If there had been an active monitoring and hunting strategy in place, analysts could have detected the anomalous behavior (e.g., unusual access to the POS system) and stopped the breach before it escalated.

In hindsight, a proactive threat hunter might have noticed the suspicious activities related to the third-party credentials being misused, flagged it as a potential threat, and taken immediate action, thereby preventing the breach.

Why Threat Hunting is Essential for Businesses

Overview of Evolving Cyber Threats (e.g., Ransomware, APTs, Insider Threats)

The threat landscape is evolving at an unprecedented rate. Traditional attacks like **viruses** and **worms** have been joined by more advanced forms of cyberattacks, such as **ransomware**, **Advanced Persistent Threats (APTs)**, and **insider threats**. These sophisticated attacks are often designed to bypass traditional security defenses and remain undetected for extended periods.

- **Ransomware**: Attackers encrypt critical data and demand a ransom in exchange for the decryption key. Examples such as the **WannaCry** and **NotPetya** ransomware attacks disrupted businesses globally, highlighting the importance of early detection and response.

- **Advanced Persistent Threats (APTs)**: These are highly sophisticated, long-term attacks often carried out by state-sponsored actors. The goal of an APT is not immediate financial gain, but rather to spy on or sabotage a target over a long period of time. APTs are stealthy and hard to detect, which is why proactive hunting is crucial.

- **Insider Threats**: Not all threats come from external sources. Employees or contractors with access to critical systems and data can be a serious security risk. Insider threats are often difficult to detect because they involve legitimate access credentials and can be conducted under the radar of traditional security measures.

Increasing Attack Surfaces Due to Digital Transformation and Remote Work

As businesses increasingly adopt cloud technologies, IoT devices, and remote work practices, the attack surface—i.e., the number of potential entry points into an organization's network—expands significantly. The digital transformation, while beneficial in many ways, introduces new vulnerabilities.

For example, the **work-from-home** trend accelerated by the COVID-19 pandemic has led to many companies relying more heavily on cloud services and remote collaboration tools. While this has enabled greater flexibility and productivity, it has also opened new opportunities for cybercriminals to exploit vulnerabilities in unpatched systems, misconfigured cloud services, or insecure remote access methods.

The **cloud environment** itself can be particularly vulnerable if businesses do not have a thorough understanding of cloud security. Many companies mistakenly believe their cloud providers will handle all security aspects, but in reality, security in the cloud is a shared responsibility, and organizations must remain vigilant about securing their environments.

Real-World Example: Case Study of an Organization that Suffered Significant Loss Due to Lack of Threat Hunting

A **well-known example** of a company that suffered significant loss due to the lack of a threat-hunting strategy is **Equifax**, one of the largest credit bureaus in the United States. In 2017, Equifax experienced a massive data breach that exposed the personal information of approximately 147 million individuals.

The breach occurred because Equifax failed to patch a **known vulnerability** in the Apache Struts web framework, which had been exploited by attackers. Despite the fact that a patch for the vulnerability had been available for months, Equifax's security team failed to address it promptly.

In this case, proactive threat hunting could have helped identify unusual activity, such as an attempted exploitation of the unpatched vulnerability, or the presence of malicious tools within the network. If the security team had actively monitored and investigated traffic and system logs, they might have detected the intrusion at an earlier stage, potentially limiting the damage and preventing the breach.

The Importance of Proactive Threat Detection

The Limitations of Traditional Cybersecurity (Firewalls, Antivirus)

Traditional cybersecurity tools—firewalls, antivirus software, and intrusion detection systems (IDS)—rely on **known signatures** and predefined rules to detect threats. These systems are highly effective at detecting attacks that have been previously identified and documented. However, they struggle to detect **new, unknown threats** or attacks that have been specifically designed to bypass these defenses.

For instance, a malware strain that uses new techniques to obfuscate its code may not be detected by signature-based antivirus software. Similarly, an advanced hacker may use techniques like **fileless malware** or **living off the land** (LOTL) tactics, which avoid detection by not writing malicious code to disk.

The Time-to-Detection Challenge in Cybersecurity Incidents

One of the biggest challenges in cybersecurity is the **time-to-detection** of threats. A study from the Ponemon Institute found that the average time it takes to detect a data breach is **197 days**. During this time, attackers can exfiltrate large volumes of sensitive data, cause significant damage to the organization's reputation, or deploy ransomware and other destructive payloads.

This delay in detection is particularly problematic when attackers use **advanced techniques** to maintain persistence in the network, such as moving laterally across systems or maintaining access through backdoors. Without proactive threat hunting, security teams often rely on automated systems to alert them to a potential breach, which may be too late to prevent significant damage.

Real-World Example: How Organizations Caught Early-Stage Attacks with Threat Hunting, Reducing Damage

A **real-world example** of early detection through threat hunting occurred at a large financial institution, where threat hunters identified unusual outbound traffic coming from an internal server. Further investigation revealed that the server had been compromised by an advanced malware variant that was attempting to exfiltrate data to a command-and-control server.

Had the organization relied solely on their firewall and antivirus software, the attack might have gone unnoticed for months. However, thanks to proactive monitoring and anomaly detection, the incident was discovered within hours, allowing the organization to shut down the compromised server and contain the damage before any sensitive data was leaked.

In this case, **threat hunting** allowed the organization to detect and respond to the attack much faster than traditional security measures would have allowed, greatly minimizing the damage and reducing the overall impact of the attack.

Threat hunting is no longer a luxury or an afterthought in cybersecurity; it's an essential strategy for organizations that want to stay ahead of increasingly sophisticated cyber threats. By proactively searching for indicators of compromise, organizations can detect attacks before they cause significant damage, mitigate risks associated with emerging threats, and ensure that their cybersecurity defenses remain effective in an ever-evolving digital landscape.

As we move forward, threat hunting will continue to play a crucial role in defending businesses from cyberattacks, and adopting it early can be the difference between a quick recovery and a catastrophic loss.

Chapter 1: Fundamentals of Cybersecurity

Basic Cybersecurity Concepts

What is a Vulnerability? What is a Threat? What is an Exploit?

In the world of cybersecurity, it's crucial to understand key concepts like **vulnerabilities**, **threats**, and **exploits**—terms that form the basis of understanding how attacks occur and how they can be mitigated.

- **Vulnerability**: A vulnerability is a weakness or flaw in a system that can potentially be exploited by a cybercriminal to gain unauthorized access or cause harm. Vulnerabilities can exist in software, hardware, or even human behavior. For instance, **unpatched software** or **poorly configured systems** are common vulnerabilities that attackers may exploit.

- **Threat**: A threat refers to any potential danger that could exploit a vulnerability and cause harm. A threat could be an individual (such as a hacker), a group, or even a natural disaster that could compromise an organization's security.

- **Exploit**: An exploit is a method or tool used by cybercriminals to take advantage of a vulnerability.

It is essentially the weapon used by an attacker to capitalize on a system's weaknesses.

Real-World Example: How a Vulnerability like "Log4Shell" Was Exploited in a Real-World Attack

A prominent real-world example of a vulnerability being exploited is the **Log4Shell vulnerability** discovered in December 2021. The **Log4Shell** flaw was a **remote code execution vulnerability** found in the **Apache Log4j** library, which is widely used in Java-based applications for logging purposes.

An attacker could exploit this vulnerability by sending a specially crafted input to a vulnerable server, which would then be logged by Log4j. This input could contain malicious code that, when logged, would be executed on the server, giving the attacker full control of the system. The flaw was particularly dangerous because it was easy to exploit and could lead to a **complete system compromise**.

Real-world attacks exploiting Log4Shell began almost immediately after the vulnerability was disclosed. Cybercriminals quickly automated their attacks, leveraging the flaw to gain access to servers in various industries, including technology, finance, and healthcare. The scale of the exploit was immense, affecting millions of devices worldwide.

In the context of **threat hunting**, proactive detection of **Log4Shell exploitation** could have saved organizations from the devastating impact of these attacks. For example, threat hunters could have identified suspicious network traffic patterns or anomalous log entries, enabling them to detect and block the attack before it caused significant harm.

Types of Cybersecurity Attacks

Cybersecurity attacks come in various forms, each with its unique methods and objectives. Understanding these types is crucial for developing effective defenses and proactive threat-hunting strategies.

- **Phishing**: Phishing is a type of attack where cybercriminals impersonate legitimate entities (e.g., banks, email providers) to trick users into revealing sensitive information, such as login credentials or financial details. Phishing attacks are typically carried out through fraudulent emails, text messages, or websites.

- **Ransomware**: Ransomware is a type of malware that encrypts a victim's files, rendering them inaccessible. The attacker then demands a ransom in exchange for the decryption key. Ransomware attacks can cripple businesses and lead to significant financial and reputational damage.

- **DDoS (Distributed Denial of Service)**: In a DDoS attack, cybercriminals flood a target system or network with excessive traffic to overwhelm its resources and make it unavailable to users. While the goal is often disruption rather than data theft, DDoS attacks can still cause significant downtime and financial loss.

- **Social Engineering**: Social engineering attacks involve manipulating individuals into divulging confidential information or performing actions that compromise security. Attackers may use psychological tactics to exploit human behavior and gain unauthorized access to systems or networks.

Real-World Example: A Phishing Attack Thwarted by Threat Hunting Techniques

One of the most famous phishing attacks targeted **Google** and **Facebook** between 2013 and 2015. A cybercriminal managed to impersonate a legitimate supplier and sent fraudulent invoices to both companies, convincing them to transfer millions of dollars. The attacker used a variety of social engineering techniques, including fake emails and documents that mimicked the supplier's branding.

However, the phishing attack was eventually discovered through **proactive threat hunting**. The company's security team noticed unusual financial transactions and began analyzing email traffic and external communications. After conducting a thorough investigation, they identified the fraudulent emails that had been used in the scam. The incident was traced back to a network of criminals operating from Eastern Europe.

Through threat hunting, security analysts were able to catch the attack before it caused further damage. They tracked the origin of the malicious activity, confirmed the phishing nature of the emails, and took immediate steps to secure the company's network and prevent additional transfers. In this case, the investigation helped mitigate financial loss and prevent further exploitation.

What Threat Actors Want

Cybercriminals operate for various motives, and understanding their goals can help organizations anticipate and defend against attacks. The motivations behind cyberattacks often determine the methods used by the attackers and the targets they choose. Common threat actors include:

- **Hackers**: Hackers can range from individuals acting out of curiosity to highly skilled cybercriminals seeking to exploit vulnerabilities for personal gain or political reasons. Hackers may target a specific organization or individual to gain access to sensitive data, disrupt services, or cause damage.

- **Insiders**: **Insiders** are individuals within an organization (e.g., employees, contractors, or business partners) who misuse their access privileges to steal data, cause harm, or sabotage systems. Insider threats can be especially difficult to detect, as they typically involve legitimate access credentials.

- **Script Kiddies**: These are less skilled individuals who use pre-written scripts or tools to carry out attacks. They often target easily exploitable systems and may not fully understand the implications of their actions. While script kiddies may not be as sophisticated as other threat actors, they still pose a significant risk.

Real-World Example: How Hackers Targeted a Company's Intellectual Property Through a Spear-Phishing Attack

A real-world example of a **spear-phishing** attack targeted at an organization's intellectual property occurred in 2017 when a group of hackers attempted to steal sensitive data from **Boeing**, a leading aerospace manufacturer. The hackers carefully crafted a spear-phishing email targeting Boeing executives, disguised as a communication from a trusted colleague. The email included a link that appeared to lead to a legitimate company site but instead directed the victim to a malicious page designed to harvest login credentials.

Once the attackers gained access to the company's internal systems, they sought to exfiltrate intellectual property related to Boeing's aircraft designs and production processes. The goal of the attackers was likely to either sell this information on the black market or use it for competitive advantage.

However, the attack was foiled when the company's threat-hunting team noticed **anomalous email traffic** and suspicious login attempts from unusual IP addresses. The threat hunters analyzed email headers and traced the phishing attempt to a malicious external server. Through prompt action, the company was able to block the phishing emails, prevent further unauthorized access, and secure its sensitive intellectual property.

This case highlights how threat-hunting techniques, such as **email traffic analysis** and **credential monitoring**, can be instrumental in detecting and stopping targeted attacks on valuable assets.

In this chapter, we introduced the foundational concepts of cybersecurity, explaining key terms such as vulnerabilities, threats, and exploits, with examples like the **Log4Shell** vulnerability. We also explored the different types of cyberattacks, from phishing and ransomware to DDoS attacks and social engineering, and how threat hunters can thwart these attacks through proactive detection. Finally, we examined the various motivations of cyber threat actors—hackers, insiders, and script kiddies—illustrating how their goals impact the methods they use in attacks, such as the **spear-phishing** attack against Boeing.

With a solid understanding of these fundamental concepts, you will be better prepared to dive deeper into the technical aspects of threat hunting and learn how to proactively defend against cyber threats in the next chapters of this book.

Chapter 2: Introduction to Threat Hunting

What is Threat Hunting?

Definition and Basic Principles: Proactive, Manual, Iterative Process

Threat hunting is a **proactive** approach to cybersecurity where trained professionals, often called **threat hunters**, actively search for hidden cyber threats within a network or system. Unlike traditional security measures, which primarily focus on **reactive** detection (such as responding to alarms triggered by antivirus software or firewalls), threat hunting involves a **manual and iterative process** of searching for potential threats that may not have been detected by automated systems.

The goal of threat hunting is to **find unknown threats**—such as **zero-day exploits, advanced persistent threats (APTs)**, or **insider threats**—before they can cause significant damage. Hunters use a combination of tools, data, and their knowledge of attacker tactics to identify suspicious activity. This process is iterative, as threat hunters continuously refine their methods based on new data and emerging threats.

Key characteristics of threat hunting include:

- **Proactivity**: Hunters are not waiting for an alert to pop up. They are actively looking for threats in systems, even if no immediate signs of an attack are visible.

- **Manual Investigation**: While automation is used to collect data, the actual hunting process requires human expertise and judgment to analyze and investigate.

- **Iteration**: Threat hunters constantly refine their approach, learning from new data and adjusting their methods over time. It's not a one-time activity but an ongoing process.

Real-World Example: How a Small Business Used Threat Hunting to Detect Malware That Slipped Past Traditional Security Measures

Let's consider a **small business** that had standard security measures in place, such as firewalls, antivirus software, and intrusion detection systems. However, despite these defenses, the company suffered from **sporadic system slowdowns** and **unusual file changes** on several workstations. The employees didn't know that malware had made its way past the traditional defenses.

The IT security team decided to engage in proactive **threat hunting** to identify the root cause of these issues. Through manual investigation and data collection (including examining system logs and endpoint data), they uncovered a **malware infection** that had slipped through the antivirus software. The malware was a **zero-day exploit**, meaning it had no known signature and had not been flagged by any previous security measures.

By utilizing **threat-hunting techniques**, such as **log analysis, network traffic inspection**, and **behavioral analysis**, the team was able to track the malware's entry point, its lateral movement within the network, and its payload. They then took immediate action to contain the infection, mitigate its impact, and prevent further compromises. Without proactive threat hunting, this attack may have gone unnoticed until much more significant damage occurred.

Key Components of Threat Hunting

Successful threat hunting requires various key components that form the foundation of the hunting process. These components include:

1. **Threat Intelligence**
2. **Data Collection**
3. **Analysis**
4. **Response**

1. Threat Intelligence

Threat intelligence involves collecting and analyzing information about emerging threats and known attacker tactics, techniques, and procedures (TTPs). This intelligence can come from various sources, such as:

- **Open-source threat intelligence feeds** (e.g., threat reports from cybersecurity organizations)
- **Internal data** from previous security incidents

- **Third-party providers** offering threat intelligence services

- **Dark web monitoring** for potential breaches or leaked data

This information helps hunters identify **patterns of attack** and create hypotheses for what might be happening inside a network.

2. Data Collection

Data collection involves gathering and storing relevant data that can help identify malicious activity. This typically includes:

- **Logs**: Logs from firewalls, servers, and applications provide a detailed history of system events and user actions, which can be used to detect abnormal behavior.

- **Network Traffic**: Monitoring network traffic allows threat hunters to spot unusual data flows, unauthorized access attempts, or signs of **lateral movement**.

- **Endpoint Data**: Examining endpoint data, such as **file changes**, **process behavior**, and **registry entries**, helps detect malware or other suspicious activities on individual devices.

3. Analysis

Once the necessary data has been collected, the next step is **analysis**. This involves using both **manual investigation** and **automated tools** to sift through the data, searching for indicators of compromise (IoCs) or anomalous behavior. Analysis can take several forms:

- **Behavioral Analysis**: Examining how systems or users behave under normal conditions and then identifying deviations from the norm (e.g., a sudden spike in data being transferred).

- **Signature-based Detection**: Comparing data to known threat signatures or patterns of attack. While this is often part of traditional security measures, it can also be used within threat hunting to verify suspicious activities.

- **Anomaly Detection**: Looking for events that are out of place, such as logins from unusual locations or a sudden increase in network traffic that doesn't match expected usage.

4. Response

After identifying a threat, the next step is a **timely response**. This involves taking actions to **contain** and **mitigate** the threat, such as:

- **Isolating infected systems** to prevent the attack from spreading.

- **Patching vulnerabilities** that the threat exploited to gain access.

- **Eradication of malware** from infected endpoints or networks.

- **Restoring data** from backups if needed, and ensuring systems return to normal operations.

Skills Required for Threat Hunting

Threat hunting requires a unique blend of technical expertise and analytical skills. While automation and security tools can assist in gathering data and identifying patterns, human expertise is crucial for effective hunting.

Key skills required for threat hunting include:

1. **Analytical Thinking**: Threat hunters must be able to process and analyze large volumes of data quickly to spot patterns or anomalies that could indicate an attack. They must be inquisitive and able to think outside the box to form hypotheses about possible threats.

2. **Problem-Solving**: Threat hunting is not a simple task of following predefined steps. Hunters often encounter new or unfamiliar attacks that require creative problem-solving and adapting techniques to different environments.

3. **Knowledge of Networking**: A strong understanding of networking protocols, traffic analysis, and network security is essential for identifying suspicious traffic patterns or detecting unauthorized communication within a network.

4. **Knowledge of Operating Systems and Security Tools**: Threat hunters need in-depth knowledge of operating systems (especially Windows, Linux, and macOS) to analyze logs, processes, and file systems. Familiarity with security tools such as **SIEM systems, endpoint detection and response**

(EDR) tools, and **network traffic analyzers** is also crucial.

5. **Knowledge of Attack Techniques**: Understanding **advanced persistent threats (APTs)**, **exploit techniques**, and the tactics used by hackers can help hunters recognize the signs of a potential attack.

Real-World Example: A Threat Hunter at a Large Enterprise Had to Learn a New Tool to Identify Advanced Persistent Threats (APT)

At a large enterprise, the security team was tasked with identifying and neutralizing a sophisticated **advanced persistent threat (APT)** that had been lurking within the network for months, undetected by traditional security measures. The threat hunters had to use a range of tools and techniques to uncover the attack.

One of the hunters, a security analyst with a strong background in network security, had never worked with **Endpoint Detection and Response (EDR)** tools before. The EDR system was essential for identifying unusual endpoint behavior, such as unusual logins, file transfers, or malware presence.

To successfully track down the APT, the hunter had to **learn how to use the new EDR tool**, analyzing the data it provided and correlating it with existing network traffic logs. After weeks of monitoring and data collection, the team discovered a pattern of unauthorized access to high-level administrative accounts, which was later traced back to a **malicious insider** using stolen credentials.

This example shows how continuously developing new skills and learning new tools is a crucial part of the threat hunter's role.

In this chapter, we explored the concept of **threat hunting**, emphasizing its proactive, manual, and iterative nature. We discussed the key components of successful threat hunting, including **threat intelligence**, **data collection**, **analysis**, and **response**. We also highlighted the critical skills required for threat hunters, including analytical thinking, knowledge of security tools, and familiarity with attack techniques. Real-world examples, such as the detection of malware in a small business and the identification of an APT in a large enterprise, helped illustrate how threat hunting can uncover threats that traditional defenses miss.

Threat hunting is not just a technical skill—it's a mindset and a continuous process that requires constant adaptation, learning, and vigilance. With the skills and techniques discussed in this chapter, you'll be better prepared to dive deeper into threat hunting and tackle real-world cybersecurity challenges in the chapters to come.

Chapter 3:
Methodologies in
Threat Hunting

The Kill Chain Model

**Explanation of the Kill Chain Model: Reconnaissance,
Weaponization, Delivery, Exploitation, Installation,
Command & Control, Action on Objectives**

The **Kill Chain** model is a widely recognized framework in
cybersecurity, used to understand and break down the
stages of a cyber attack. The model was originally
developed by Lockheed Martin to help identify and prevent
attacks, particularly in military contexts, but it has since
been adapted for broader cybersecurity use. In threat
hunting, the Kill Chain offers a structured way to map out
the various steps in a cyber attack, from the initial stages of
reconnaissance to the final actions that lead to a successful
attack.

The stages of the Kill Chain are as follows:

1. **Reconnaissance**: The attacker gathers information
   about the target, identifying potential vulnerabilities
   and weaknesses. This could involve activities such
   as scanning for open ports, gathering data on
   employees, or researching the organization's
   infrastructure.

2. **Weaponization**: The attacker combines an exploit with a payload to create a malicious weapon. This could be a piece of malware, a phishing email with a malicious attachment, or a script designed to take advantage of a vulnerability.

3. **Delivery**: The weaponized exploit is delivered to the target system. This could be through email (phishing), malicious websites, infected USB devices, or network vulnerabilities.

4. **Exploitation**: The attacker exploits a vulnerability in the target system, allowing them to gain unauthorized access. This could involve exploiting a software flaw, misconfigured systems, or weak credentials.

5. **Installation**: Once access is gained, the attacker installs malware on the target system, allowing for persistence. This could be backdoors, remote access Trojans (RATs), or other malicious software that enables continued access.

6. **Command & Control (C&C)**: The attacker establishes communication with the compromised system, enabling them to send commands and receive data. This communication is often hidden, such as through encrypted channels, to avoid detection.

7. **Action on Objectives**: Finally, the attacker achieves their goal, whether it's stealing data, disrupting services, or executing other malicious activities such as ransomware attacks.

Each stage of the Kill Chain provides an opportunity for threat hunters to detect and stop the attack before it reaches its final objective. The earlier an attack is intercepted, the less damage it can cause.

Real-World Example: Walkthrough of an Attack Where Threat Hunters Used the Kill Chain to Trace the Attack's Origins

Let's consider a **phishing attack** that targeted a medium-sized corporation. The threat hunters used the Kill Chain model to investigate the incident and understand the attack's progression.

1. **Reconnaissance**: The attackers first conducted research on the target company. They discovered that employees often used a particular software suite, and they identified key personnel, including senior executives, who had access to sensitive data.

2. **Weaponization**: The attackers created a spear-phishing email disguised as a legitimate communication from the software vendor. The email contained a link that, when clicked, led to a **malicious payload** disguised as a software update.

3. **Delivery**: The phishing email was sent to the senior executives in the company. One of them clicked on the link, and the malware began downloading onto their system.

4. **Exploitation**: The malware exploited a vulnerability in the system's browser, allowing the attackers to gain access to the network without triggering any alarms from traditional antivirus software.

5. **Installation**: Once inside, the attackers installed a **remote access Trojan (RAT)**, allowing them to maintain persistent access to the network.

6. **Command & Control**: The RAT allowed the attackers to communicate with their infected system, sending commands to steal sensitive information from the company's internal databases.

7. **Action on Objectives**: The attackers eventually exfiltrated sensitive financial records and intellectual property, which they planned to sell on the dark web.

By mapping the attack using the Kill Chain model, the threat hunters were able to identify key points where they could have detected and halted the attack. For example, the initial phishing email could have been flagged by email filters, or the RAT installation could have been detected through network traffic analysis.

MITRE ATT&CK Framework

Introduction to MITRE ATT&CK: Mapping Adversarial Tactics, Techniques, and Procedures (TTPs)

The **MITRE ATT&CK** (Adversarial Tactics, Techniques, and Common Knowledge) framework is a knowledge base that describes the actions and behaviors of cyber adversaries during an attack. It is an open-source resource used by cybersecurity professionals to improve detection, analysis, and response strategies.

The ATT&CK framework is organized into a matrix, with columns representing **tactics** (the adversary's goals) and rows representing **techniques** (the methods used to achieve those goals). The matrix covers tactics such as initial access, execution, persistence, privilege escalation, defense evasion, credential access, discovery, lateral movement, collection, exfiltration, and impact.

For example:

- **Tactic: Initial Access**
  - ○ **Technique: Phishing** (Delivering a malicious payload through email)
- **Tactic: Execution**
  - ○ **Technique: PowerShell** (Using PowerShell scripts to execute commands on a compromised system)

The framework helps map **adversarial tactics, techniques, and procedures (TTPs)**, giving cybersecurity teams a structured way to understand and predict attack patterns. By mapping these TTPs, organizations can better understand how adversaries work and apply the appropriate countermeasures.

Real-World Example: Case Study on How MITRE ATT&CK Was Used to Identify a Threat Actor's Actions

In this case, let's consider a **ransomware attack** that was detected in its early stages due to the use of the MITRE ATT&CK framework. The attackers initially gained access to the system via **phishing** (Tactic: Initial Access, Technique: Spear-phishing Attachment). Once inside, they began to **escalate their privileges** using tools like **Mimikatz** (Tactic: Privilege Escalation, Technique: Credentials Dumping).

The threat hunters used MITRE ATT&CK to map the adversary's TTPs. They identified that the attackers were attempting to move laterally across the network using **Windows Management Instrumentation (WMI)** (Tactic: Lateral Movement, Technique: WMI). By using MITRE ATT&CK's detailed matrix, the hunters were able to quickly correlate these tactics with previous threat actor behavior patterns and prevent the attackers from gaining further control over critical systems.

The use of the MITRE ATT&CK framework allowed the security team to **prioritize** their investigations, based on the **most likely tactics and techniques** that the attackers would employ next. This proactive approach helped them thwart the attack before it escalated into a full ransomware deployment.

Hunt Cycles and Investigation

The Hunt Cycle: Hypothesis, Data Collection, Analysis, and Response

The **hunt cycle** is the core process that drives threat hunting. It involves four key steps:

1. **Hypothesis**: The process begins with the formulation of a hypothesis, which is a suspected scenario or theory about possible malicious activity within the network. The hypothesis could be based

on a **pattern recognition** or the **analysis of unusual behavior**.

For example, a hunter might hypothesize that an employee's account has been compromised because there was an unexpected login from a foreign country.

2. **Data Collection**: Once a hypothesis is formed, the next step is to gather relevant data to test the hypothesis. This could involve collecting logs, network traffic, endpoint data, or system configurations that could provide insights into whether the suspected threat is real.

In the case of the employee's compromised account, the hunter might collect login history, IP geolocation data, and other endpoint activity logs to confirm if there is any unusual behavior.

3. **Analysis**: After collecting the necessary data, the next step is to analyze it to identify **indicators of compromise (IoCs)** or **patterns of malicious activity**. This phase requires careful inspection of the data, often using security tools, and may involve using the MITRE ATT&CK framework to identify potential attack techniques.

4. **Response**: Finally, if the analysis confirms the presence of a threat, the hunter must respond by neutralizing the threat. This could involve actions such as **isolating infected systems, removing malware**, or **blocking malicious IP addresses**.

Real-World Example: How an Initial Hypothesis About Abnormal Traffic Led to a Full-Scale Investigation

In a corporate environment, abnormal **network traffic spikes** were noticed on certain internal servers. A **hypothesis** was formed: "The network traffic could be indicative of **data exfiltration** or a potential **malware** communication with a command-and-control server."

The next step was **data collection**: the hunters gathered network traffic logs, including packet captures and server logs, to determine the nature of the traffic.

Through **analysis**, it was discovered that the traffic was unusual because it was encrypted and coming from a server that shouldn't have been making external communication. The hunters used **network analysis tools** to trace the traffic back to an external IP address known to be used by a botnet.

Finally, the hunters **responded** by blocking the suspicious IP, quarantining the affected servers, and conducting a deeper investigation to uncover the full scope of the attack, preventing data exfiltration and further damage.

In this chapter, we explored several key methodologies used in threat hunting: the **Kill Chain model**, the **MITRE ATT&CK framework**, and the **hunt cycle**. Each of these methodologies provides a structured approach to understanding and detecting cyber threats, helping organizations proactively defend against malicious activity.

Key Takeaways:

- The **Kill Chain** model helps trace an attack's origins and identifies points where defense measures can be applied.

- The **MITRE ATT&CK framework** provides a comprehensive matrix of adversarial tactics, techniques, and procedures, helping to map and predict cyberattack behavior.

- The **hunt cycle** involves formulating hypotheses, collecting data, analyzing evidence, and responding to threats, forming the basis of a proactive threat-hunting strategy.

Chapter 4: Tools and Technologies for Threat Hunting

Common Threat Hunting Tools

Effective **threat hunting** relies heavily on the use of specialized tools that help detect, investigate, and respond to security incidents. These tools help security professionals gather and analyze data, identify indicators of compromise (IoCs), and enhance their ability to uncover potential threats that bypass traditional defenses. Here are some of the most commonly used tools in the world of threat hunting:

1. SIEM (Security Information and Event Management)

SIEM systems are integral to modern cybersecurity operations. They gather, aggregate, and analyze security data from across an organization's IT infrastructure, helping security teams detect, investigate, and respond to potential threats. SIEM tools collect log data from network devices, endpoints, servers, and applications, and then use advanced analytics to identify patterns that may indicate a security incident.

- **Key Features**:

- Log Aggregation: SIEM systems collect logs from various sources in real-time.

- Correlation: SIEM systems analyze data to correlate events, providing insights into potential attack patterns.

- Alerting: Automated alerts are generated when suspicious behavior is detected.

Real-World Example: Using SIEM Tools to Detect Unusual Network Traffic in a Cloud Environment

A company operating a cloud-based infrastructure noticed a sudden spike in outbound network traffic from one of their critical servers, which had not been observed before. The security team used their SIEM platform to collect network traffic logs and other security event data.

Upon investigating, they identified a pattern where an unauthorized external server had been communicating with an internal application, suggesting possible **data exfiltration**. The SIEM tool correlated this event with other suspicious behavior, such as a sudden rise in privileged access logs, which led the team to quickly identify the attack.

Thanks to the SIEM system's real-time alerts, the threat was contained before any significant data loss occurred. The SIEM tool helped the security team correlate multiple data points, providing clear evidence of the attack and enabling a swift response.

2. EDR (Endpoint Detection and Response)

EDR tools focus on monitoring and responding to threats on individual endpoints (e.g., workstations, laptops, mobile devices). These tools provide deep visibility into endpoint activities, enabling security teams to detect malicious behavior that may not be caught by traditional antivirus software.

- **Key Features**:
    - **Continuous Monitoring**: EDR tools constantly monitor endpoint activity for unusual behavior.
    - **Malware Detection**: EDR tools identify known and unknown malware using signature-based and behavior-based methods.
    - **Forensic Analysis**: EDR tools allow security teams to review historical data from endpoints, providing context for potential attacks.

Real-World Example: Using EDR to Detect Malware on an Employee Laptop

In a recent incident, an employee's laptop was compromised by malware after opening a phishing email. The malware went undetected by traditional antivirus software but was picked up by the company's **EDR solution**, which continuously monitored the endpoint.

The EDR system flagged suspicious activity when the malware attempted to execute a PowerShell script to download additional payloads. The security team used the EDR tool to isolate the laptop from the network and then conducted a deeper investigation. They found that the malware was attempting to communicate with an external server, confirming the presence of an advanced threat.

By using the **EDR tool**, the team was able to quickly contain the threat, removing the malware and restoring the endpoint to a secure state before the attacker could escalate the attack further.

How to Use Logs and Data Feeds

Logs are crucial to the **threat hunting** process, as they provide detailed records of system and network activity that can be analyzed for indicators of compromise (IoCs). By examining logs, threat hunters can identify unusual behavior, track an attacker's movements, and gather evidence for further investigation.

1. Types of Logs Commonly Used in Threat Hunting

- **Windows Event Logs**: These logs contain critical information about system events, user activities, and security events. They are often the first place threat hunters look for signs of malicious activity.

- **Network Logs**: Network devices such as routers and firewalls generate logs that show traffic patterns, failed connection attempts, and potential breaches.

- **Application Logs**: These logs provide details on how applications behave and can be helpful in detecting anomalous application behavior.

- **Authentication Logs**: These logs show information about user logins and authentication attempts. Failed login attempts or unusual login times are important red flags.

Real-World Example: Analyzing Windows Event Logs to Uncover an Insider Threat

A financial services company experienced an unusual spike in login attempts during off-hours, which triggered an alert in their SIEM tool. Upon further investigation, the threat hunters examined the **Windows Event Logs** for evidence of **privilege escalation** or unusual access patterns.

The logs revealed that an employee had accessed sensitive financial records outside their normal work hours and from a device that had not been previously used. The security team identified that the employee's credentials had been compromised by an insider threat, allowing unauthorized access.

This early detection allowed the company to respond before the attacker could cause significant damage, including financial theft. The hunters were able to correlate login data with file access logs, identifying the scope of the breach and limiting its impact.

Advanced Tools for Threat Hunting

As cyber threats evolve and become more sophisticated, organizations often require advanced tools to stay ahead. These tools provide more in-depth analysis and enable hunters to detect and mitigate complex attacks like advanced persistent threats (APTs), zero-day vulnerabilities, and other sophisticated techniques.

1. Threat Intelligence Platforms

Threat intelligence platforms aggregate, analyze, and disseminate information about current and emerging threats. They collect data from a variety of sources, such as government agencies, cybersecurity vendors, and the dark web, to provide real-time information on new attack techniques, IoCs, and threat actor activities.

- **Key Features**:
  - **Real-time Threat Feeds**: Continuous updates on emerging threats, vulnerabilities, and attack tactics.
  - **Automated Indicators**: Automated alerts on newly discovered IoCs, such as malicious IPs, domain names, and hashes.
  - **Enrichment**: Enriching threat data by providing context about threat actors, their tactics, and their methods.

Real-World Example: Using Threat Intelligence to Detect a New Type of Attack

A large multinational company was targeted by a **new type of ransomware attack** that had not been seen before. The attack bypassed traditional security defenses, and the organization's SIEM and EDR tools initially failed to detect it.

Fortunately, the company had integrated a **threat intelligence platform** into its security operations. The platform provided information on a **new ransomware**

variant that had been detected in other regions. By using the intelligence from the platform, the security team was able to correlate data from their logs and identify the initial signs of the attack, which had started spreading through the network.

The platform's real-time updates helped the team detect the attack early, before it could cause widespread damage. The threat intelligence tool also provided the team with **indicators of compromise** specific to the ransomware, which helped them isolate infected systems and block communication with the attacker's command and control servers.

2. Network Traffic Analysis Tools

Network traffic analysis tools help threat hunters monitor network behavior and identify potential malicious activity, such as data exfiltration, unauthorized access, and lateral movement. These tools analyze **network traffic patterns** to detect anomalies that may signal a compromise.

- **Key Features**:
    - **Deep Packet Inspection**: Analyzing the content of network packets to detect hidden threats.
    - **Traffic Anomaly Detection**: Identifying unusual traffic patterns, such as spikes in outbound data or communications with known malicious IP addresses.

o **Protocol Analysis**: Understanding the specific protocols used in network communications to detect protocol abuse.

Real-World Example: Using Network Traffic Analysis to Detect Lateral Movement

In a corporate network, network traffic analysis tools helped detect **lateral movement** by an attacker who had gained access through an employee's compromised credentials. The attacker was attempting to move from the initial compromised system to other devices on the network.

By monitoring the network traffic, the hunters identified unusual patterns of communication between devices that were not normally in contact with each other. The analysis also revealed **SSH tunneling**, where the attacker was trying to disguise their traffic to avoid detection.

Using the **network traffic analysis tools**, the security team was able to trace the attack's progression, identify the compromised systems, and contain the threat before any critical data was stolen.

In this chapter, we explored the various tools and technologies that play a vital role in **threat hunting**. These tools enable security teams to detect, investigate, and mitigate cyber threats effectively, providing essential insights into malicious activity.

Key Takeaways:

- **SIEM** and **EDR** tools are fundamental for real-time monitoring, analysis, and response to security incidents.

- **Logs and data feeds** are crucial for uncovering IoCs and detecting threats that evade traditional defenses.

- Advanced tools like **Threat Intelligence platforms**, **network traffic analysis tools**, and **malware analysis tools** provide in-depth insights and enable proactive defense strategies against sophisticated attacks.

Chapter 5: Building a Threat Hunting Strategy

Creating a robust **threat hunting strategy** is crucial for organizations that want to proactively identify and mitigate cybersecurity risks. While threat hunting can be a complex and resource-intensive process, with the right approach, even small organizations can build an effective program tailored to their needs. This chapter will guide you through the steps of developing a threat hunting strategy, setting up an effective team, and integrating threat hunting into your broader cybersecurity programs.

Creating a Threat Hunting Plan

A **threat hunting plan** is the foundation of any successful threat hunting program. It defines the organization's approach to proactively detecting threats, establishing clear objectives, and aligning tools and resources to achieve these goals. A well-structured plan helps streamline the hunting process and ensures the team remains focused and efficient.

Steps to Design a Comprehensive Threat Hunting Strategy

1. **Define Objectives**

   o **What are you hunting for?** Are you focused on detecting advanced persistent threats (APTs), insider threats, malware, or unusual network traffic? Define clear goals for the hunt, based on your organization's risk profile and existing security gaps.

   o **Focus on high-risk areas:** Prioritize areas that are most critical to your organization, such as intellectual property, customer data, or financial records.

2. **Select Tools and Resources**

   o **Tools for Collection and Analysis:** Choose the right combination of tools (SIEM, EDR, threat intelligence platforms, etc.) based on your needs. Consider factors like network architecture, endpoint coverage, and the type of data your tools will need to analyze.

   o **Resource Allocation:** Determine the human and technological resources available to your team. Resources can range from budget and tools to skilled personnel.

3. **Create a Hypothesis-Driven Approach**

   o Begin with a hypothesis of potential threats based on past incidents, current vulnerabilities, or emerging attack trends. This helps focus your hunting activities on likely attack vectors.

- o **Data Collection:** Use your hypothesis to guide data collection. For example, if you suspect an insider threat, you may focus on user login and file access logs.

4. **Establish Metrics for Success**

- o **Performance Indicators:** Establish key performance indicators (KPIs) for your threat-hunting efforts, such as detection time, false positive rate, or time-to-containment.

- o **Continuous Improvement:** Use metrics to assess the effectiveness of your strategy and refine your hunting processes over time.

Real-World Example: A Small Company Building a Threat-Hunting Program with Limited Resources

A small financial firm with limited resources wanted to implement a basic threat-hunting program. Although the company lacked a dedicated cybersecurity team and had a limited budget, they focused on the most critical assets: customer data and financial records.

- **Objective:** They defined their hunting objectives around detecting insider threats and advanced malware targeting their financial systems.

- **Tools:** The firm used an affordable SIEM tool that was easy to configure and could integrate with their existing endpoint detection software. They also leveraged open-source threat intelligence feeds.

- **Team and Resources:** With a small team of two IT professionals and one outsourced security consultant, they were able to create basic hunting hypotheses based on known attack patterns in the financial sector. By focusing on log collection, user behavior analysis, and network traffic monitoring, they were able to identify and neutralize a phishing attack before it spread.

Despite their limited resources, the company was able to build an effective and cost-conscious threat-hunting program by focusing on essential tools and objectives.

Setting Up a Threat Hunting Team

A well-structured **threat hunting team** is vital for the success of any hunting operation. The team needs to be equipped with the right skills, tools, and resources to detect, investigate, and respond to threats efficiently.

Essential Roles in a Threat Hunting Team

1. **Threat Hunters**

   - These are the individuals responsible for leading the hunting activities. They proactively search for indicators of compromise (IoCs), suspicious behavior, and emerging threats within the organization's systems.

   - **Skills Required:** A deep understanding of network protocols, system administration, threat actor behaviors, and security tools.

2. **Security Analysts**

- Analysts assist threat hunters by analyzing the data collected during hunts. They look for patterns, anomalies, and correlations to support the team's investigations.

- **Skills Required:** Analytical thinking, experience with security operations, and proficiency in using SIEM and other security tools.

3. **Incident Responders**

- Incident responders take action once a threat has been detected. Their job is to contain the attack, mitigate damage, and support recovery efforts.

- **Skills Required:** Experience with incident response protocols, knowledge of forensic analysis, and skills in containment and remediation.

4. **Supporting Roles**

- **Cybersecurity Engineers** ensure that the necessary tools and systems are in place and functioning properly.

- **Risk Managers** help assess the business impact of detected threats and guide prioritization based on the organization's risk tolerance.

Real-World Example: How a Cybersecurity Team of 3 Was Able to Secure a Company Using Collaborative Threat Hunting

A mid-sized company with a cybersecurity team of just three people set out to implement a threat-hunting strategy. Despite their small size, the team utilized collaboration and a structured workflow to ensure success.

- **Team Structure**:
    - The **lead threat hunter** focused on analyzing network traffic and hunting for advanced persistent threats (APTs).
    - The **security analyst** handled data collection, including log aggregation and analysis, and assisted with event correlation.
    - The **incident responder** was primarily responsible for containment and remediation once a threat was identified.
- **Collaboration:** The team developed a close-knit workflow where the threat hunter created hypotheses, the analyst collected and analyzed data, and the responder worked with both to ensure rapid action when necessary. This approach allowed them to efficiently hunt for threats, despite their small team size.

In one particular instance, the team was able to detect a **phishing attack** targeting several employees. The threat hunter identified suspicious email traffic using the SIEM tool, and the analyst quickly correlated this with login attempts on several internal systems. The incident responder immediately initiated an isolation process for the compromised systems, preventing the attack from spreading further.

By effectively communicating and working together, this small team was able to detect, investigate, and contain the attack before it caused significant harm.

Integrating Threat Hunting with Other Security Programs

For threat hunting to be effective, it must be integrated into a broader security strategy. Threat hunting cannot operate in isolation but should work in tandem with other essential cybersecurity functions, such as **vulnerability management**, **incident response**, and **risk management**.

How Threat Hunting Works Alongside Other Security Programs

1. **Vulnerability Management**

    o   Threat hunting can help identify unpatched vulnerabilities that could be exploited by attackers. By hunting proactively, security teams can prioritize patching efforts based on identified threats and vulnerabilities.

    o   **Example**: A vulnerability management program may be used to patch systems, while threat hunting focuses on identifying whether the unpatched vulnerability is already being exploited in the network.

2. **Incident Response**

    o   Threat hunting provides valuable intelligence that can help incident responders quickly identify and respond to active threats. Effective hunting often involves real-time alerts and early detection that lead to faster containment and mitigation.

- o **Example**: An incident response plan may kick in after a threat hunting activity uncovers signs of an attack, such as unusual behavior or unauthorized access.

3. **Risk Management**

- o Threat hunting feeds into the risk management process by identifying emerging threats that could impact the organization's risk profile. Early detection allows risk managers to assess the potential impact of threats and guide decision-making on how to allocate resources for prevention and mitigation.

- o **Example**: A new attack vector identified during threat hunting could trigger a reassessment of risk, leading to changes in security posture or resource allocation.

Real-World Example: How an Integrated Approach Led to Early Detection and Rapid Mitigation

A large retail chain integrated its **threat hunting** efforts with its vulnerability management and incident response programs. When a **Zero-Day vulnerability** was discovered in one of their web applications, threat hunters immediately began scanning for any exploitation of the flaw within their network.

They were able to detect abnormal behavior on an affected server, which was linked to the Zero-Day exploit. The threat-hunting team worked closely with the incident response team to isolate the server, preventing further exploitation.

Simultaneously, the **vulnerability management team** began working on patching the application. This integration of efforts allowed the company to contain the threat rapidly while minimizing damage and exposure.

Building an effective threat-hunting strategy involves defining clear objectives, selecting appropriate tools, creating a skilled team, and ensuring coordination with other security functions. A well-structured program is key to identifying and mitigating threats before they can cause significant damage.

Key Takeaways:

- **Creating a Threat Hunting Plan**: Define objectives, select tools, and establish metrics for success.

- **Setting Up a Threat Hunting Team**: Build a collaborative team of threat hunters, analysts, and incident responders.

- **Integrating Threat Hunting with Other Security Programs**: Align threat hunting with vulnerability management, incident response, and risk management for a comprehensive defense strategy.

Chapter 6: Data Collection and Analysis for Threat Hunting

In the world of cybersecurity, effective **data collection** and **analysis** are at the heart of any successful **threat hunting** operation. To proactively detect and mitigate threats, threat hunters must gather relevant data from a variety of sources, analyze it for signs of suspicious activity, and correlate multiple events to identify sophisticated or multi-stage attacks. This chapter focuses on the methods and best practices for collecting, analyzing, and correlating data during threat hunting.

Gathering Data from Multiple Sources

Effective threat hunting relies on gathering data from various sources to create a comprehensive view of the organization's network and systems. Data collection allows threat hunters to identify indicators of compromise (IoCs), track unusual behaviors, and uncover malicious activity that may otherwise go undetected by traditional security tools.

Key Sources of Data for Threat Hunting

1. **Endpoints**:

    o   Endpoints (such as workstations, servers, and mobile devices) provide crucial data that can reveal malicious activity. This includes **file access logs**, **process information**, **registry changes**, and **user activity logs**.

    o   By monitoring endpoint data, hunters can look for signs of malware, unauthorized access, or abnormal behavior at the device level.

2. **Network Traffic**:

    o   Network traffic provides insight into the data being transferred across an organization's network. Threat hunters can analyze **packet captures (PCAPs)**, **flow data**, **traffic logs**, and **network behavior** to identify unusual connections, patterns, or data transfers.

    o   **Network behavior analysis** can help detect anomalies that indicate a compromise, such as unusual communication with external IP addresses or data exfiltration attempts.

3. **Security Logs**:

    o   Logs from various security tools (e.g., **firewalls**, **intrusion detection systems**, **antivirus programs**, **SIEM** solutions) are rich sources of data. These logs often contain timestamps, IP addresses, system alerts, and details of potential attacks or system anomalies.

o By analyzing these logs, threat hunters can uncover patterns of malicious activity, such as brute-force attacks or unauthorized access attempts.

4. **Threat Intelligence Feeds**:

o Threat intelligence feeds provide external sources of information about emerging threats, indicators of compromise, and the tactics, techniques, and procedures (TTPs) used by threat actors. These feeds can be used to compare against the internal data being collected to identify known threats or attack patterns.

o Incorporating threat intelligence allows hunters to stay ahead of new attack trends, improving the chances of detecting threats before they escalate.

Real-World Example: How a Team Collected Network Traffic Data to Identify Unusual External Connections

A financial institution was concerned about potential data exfiltration attempts from its internal network. The organization had deployed basic security measures, but they wanted to enhance their threat-hunting capabilities.

- The **threat-hunting team** started by collecting **network traffic logs** to monitor connections to and from their internal network. They used **network traffic analysis tools** to examine the flow of data between internal devices and external servers.

- **Findings**: During the analysis, they identified unusual **outbound traffic** to an **IP address** that was not associated with any known business relationship. The traffic was unusually large and occurred during off-hours, suggesting a potential attempt to exfiltrate sensitive financial data.

- The team escalated the investigation and found that a **compromised employee workstation** was making these unusual connections. They quickly isolated the affected system and prevented further data transfer.

By collecting network traffic data and analyzing it for anomalies, the team was able to detect a potential data exfiltration attack before any damage occurred.

Analyzing Suspicious Activity

Once data is collected, the next crucial step is to **analyze** it for **suspicious activity**. This process often involves looking for **anomalies** that deviate from normal system behavior. Effective analysis relies on a deep understanding of what "normal" looks like and what kinds of activities are indicative of a threat.

Key Techniques for Analyzing Suspicious Activity

1. **Pattern Recognition**:

- Threat hunters look for known patterns of malicious activity, such as familiar IoCs (IP addresses, file hashes, domain names) or typical attack signatures. This might involve comparing collected data to databases of known malware or attack patterns.

2. **Baselines and Normal Behavior**:

- Establishing a **baseline** of normal network behavior is crucial to spotting deviations. For example, if an employee usually logs in at certain times and accesses specific resources, any deviation (e.g., a login attempt at an unusual hour or accessing unfamiliar systems) could be flagged for further investigation.

- **Behavioral analysis** can also help identify threats that don't rely on known patterns but instead exhibit abnormal behavior. For example, a user accessing an unusually high number of files or making an unusually large number of network requests might signal malicious activity.

3. **Anomaly Detection**:

- Anomaly detection focuses on spotting deviations from the norm that could indicate malicious behavior. This can include high volumes of data being transferred to unknown destinations or an endpoint exhibiting behavior that doesn't match the user's usual patterns.

- Tools like **UEBA (User and Entity Behavior Analytics)** can help automate the identification of behavioral anomalies that may not be immediately obvious through traditional log analysis.

Real-World Example: How Abnormal DNS Requests Were Used to Detect a Data Exfiltration Attack

A large e-commerce company was concerned about potential data exfiltration attempts via DNS tunneling, a technique where data is exfiltrated by encoding it in DNS queries.

- The company's **threat-hunting team** began monitoring **DNS request logs** for unusual activity, as DNS requests are typically allowed through firewalls.

- **Findings**: They noticed a high volume of DNS requests with unusually long payloads being sent to an external domain. This was an anomaly compared to typical DNS queries, which are usually much shorter.

- Upon further investigation, the team discovered that an **internal server** had been compromised and was using DNS queries to tunnel out sensitive data to an attacker-controlled server.

- By identifying these abnormal DNS requests, the team was able to stop the data exfiltration and shut down the compromised server.

This example highlights how analyzing unusual activity at the protocol level—such as DNS—can reveal sophisticated attack methods like DNS tunneling.

Correlating Events and Indicators

Correlating data from multiple sources is a powerful technique in threat hunting. Attackers often use multiple stages and techniques to carry out their objectives, making it necessary to combine various data points to uncover the full scope of an attack.

Techniques for Correlating Events

1. **Cross-Referencing Logs**:

     o By comparing data from different sources, threat hunters can often uncover a more complete picture of an attack. For example, combining **firewall logs, user authentication logs**, and **network traffic data** might reveal a multi-stage attack where an attacker first gains access via a compromised user account and then establishes communication with an external server.

2. **Connecting the Dots**:

     o Attackers often use multiple techniques across different systems to maintain persistence. Correlating events allows threat hunters to follow the trail of an attack, from initial compromise to eventual exfiltration or system manipulation.

- Correlation can also help identify lateral movement, where attackers move from one compromised system to another within the network.

Real-World Example: How Failed Login Attempts Combined with Suspicious Traffic Helped Pinpoint a Targeted Attack

A large technology company noticed that several employees were receiving suspicious login attempts from an external IP address. While this alone was not enough to raise alarm, the company's threat-hunting team decided to investigate further.

- The team examined the **failed login attempts** in combination with **network traffic data** and found that the failed login attempts were followed by unusual outbound traffic to the same IP address.

- This correlation suggested that the attacker was attempting to brute-force their way into internal systems before establishing a connection for data exfiltration.

- The **event correlation** between failed logins and suspicious traffic led the team to identify the attack's origin and stop it before the attacker could achieve their objective.

This case illustrates how correlating seemingly unrelated events (failed logins and suspicious network traffic) can help detect a targeted attack that may not be immediately obvious from a single data source.

Effective **data collection** and **analysis** are central to identifying and responding to cyber threats. By gathering data from multiple sources such as **endpoints, network traffic, security logs**, and **threat intelligence feeds**, threat hunters can build a comprehensive picture of what's happening in their organization's network. Through the application of techniques like **pattern recognition, baseline analysis**, and **anomaly detection**, hunters can spot suspicious activity early and respond swiftly.

Key Takeaways:

- **Data Collection**: Gather data from multiple sources to uncover potential threats.

- **Analyzing Suspicious Activity**: Use pattern recognition, baselines, and anomaly detection to spot unusual behavior.

- **Correlating Events**: Combine different data points to uncover multi-stage attacks and gain deeper insights into an attack's progression.

Chapter 7: Techniques for Effective Threat Hunting

In this chapter, we explore various **techniques** that threat hunters use to detect and mitigate cybersecurity threats effectively. The approach to threat hunting is often not linear but iterative, relying on critical thinking, pattern recognition, and the utilization of advanced tools. The techniques outlined in this chapter aim to enhance the effectiveness of threat hunting operations, enabling organizations to proactively identify emerging threats, prevent attacks, and minimize damage. We'll dive into **hypothesis-driven hunting, behavioral analysis techniques**, and the role of **machine learning** in modern threat hunting.

Hypothesis-Driven Hunting

Hypothesis-driven threat hunting is a method in which hunters use a well-formed **hypothesis** to guide their search for specific indicators of compromise (IoCs) or suspicious activity within a network. This method allows hunters to focus their efforts on specific behaviors, patterns, or tactics, making their investigations more efficient and targeted.

Crafting a Hypothesis Based on Known Threat Intelligence or Anomalous Activity

- **Start with a Suspicious Event**: A hypothesis is typically built when there is an observable anomaly or a pattern of activity that may suggest an attack. Threat intelligence, previous incidents, or known adversarial tactics can provide insight into what could be happening inside a network.

- **Formulating the Hypothesis**: The hypothesis should focus on specific behaviors or indicators that, if found, would confirm the presence of a threat. For example, a hypothesis could be: "If there are multiple failed login attempts followed by unusual file access on an internal server, this might indicate a potential brute-force attack followed by lateral movement."

- **Testing the Hypothesis**: Threat hunters will test their hypothesis by gathering and analyzing relevant data, such as logs, endpoint activities, and network traffic. If the hypothesis proves true, they can proceed with further investigation or mitigation efforts.

Real-World Example: How a Hypothesis About Unusual File Access Led to the Discovery of a Data Breach

A financial services company had recently implemented new security measures to protect customer data. A few weeks after the new protocols were established, the **security team** noticed unusual access patterns within the internal network. Specifically, certain files were being accessed more frequently by employees who didn't normally interact with those files.

- The team developed a **hypothesis**: "Unusual access patterns on sensitive files could indicate unauthorized access, potentially leading to a data breach."

- They tested this hypothesis by reviewing **file access logs**, **authentication logs**, and **network traffic data**. Their analysis revealed that one employee's credentials were being used to access large volumes of customer data, even though the employee had no legitimate reason to do so.

- After further investigation, it was determined that the employee's account had been **compromised**, and the attacker was using it to extract sensitive financial data from the network. The breach was contained before significant damage occurred, thanks to the proactive hypothesis-driven hunting method.

Behavioral Analysis Techniques

Behavioral analysis is the practice of identifying threats by studying abnormal or malicious behavior patterns, rather than relying solely on known attack signatures. This approach allows threat hunters to detect previously unknown threats, such as **zero-day vulnerabilities** or new types of **advanced persistent threats (APTs)**.

Detecting Threats by Analyzing Behavior Rather Than Relying on Signatures

1. **Baseline Behavior**:

   o The first step in behavioral analysis is to establish a baseline of what normal activity looks like in the organization. This could include patterns of **user activity**, **network traffic**, **file access**, or **system processes**.

   o Once a baseline is established, deviations from this normal behavior—such as a user accessing files at odd hours or unusually high data transfers—can be flagged as suspicious.

2. **User and Entity Behavior Analytics (UEBA)**:

   o **UEBA tools** are designed to analyze both user and entity (devices, systems, or network traffic) behavior and spot unusual patterns that may suggest malicious activity. This analysis typically involves machine learning and statistical algorithms to identify anomalies based on historical data.

   o For example, a UEBA system might flag an employee's account if it suddenly begins downloading a massive amount of files, accessing resources not typically used, or communicating with unfamiliar external IP addresses.

Real-World Example: How Pattern Analysis in User Behavior Helped Identify a Malware Infection

A **large healthcare organization** used behavioral analysis to detect a malware infection that had bypassed traditional security measures. The malware was **undetected by antivirus software** but exhibited clear signs of malicious behavior.

- The **threat-hunting team** used **UEBA tools** to analyze user activity across the network. One particular user, who typically worked during business hours and accessed a specific set of medical records, began to exhibit abnormal behavior—accessing records at odd times and connecting to unfamiliar network shares.

- Upon further investigation, the team discovered that the user's credentials had been compromised, and an attacker had used them to install a piece of malware on the system. This malware was silently spreading across the network, trying to gain higher privileges and exfiltrate sensitive data.

- **Behavioral analysis** helped identify the abnormal activity, leading to a swift response that quarantined the infected systems and removed the malware before it could cause significant damage.

Using Machine Learning in Threat Hunting

Machine learning (ML) and artificial intelligence (AI) are revolutionizing the way threat hunters detect and mitigate threats. By leveraging vast amounts of data and learning from previous attack patterns, machine learning algorithms can spot anomalies faster and more accurately than traditional methods.

How Machine Learning and AI Can Augment Threat Hunting Efforts

1. **Automated Detection**:

   o Machine learning algorithms can process vast amounts of data in real time, looking for patterns and anomalies that may indicate an attack. For instance, ML tools can detect unusual network traffic, file access patterns, or login behaviors by learning what is "normal" within the network environment.

   o These systems can also continuously learn from new data, improving their detection capabilities over time and adapting to changing attack tactics.

2. **Threat Classification**:

   o ML can classify threats based on historical data. For example, it can recognize **malicious** file hashes or **IP addresses** that match known attack signatures and automatically raise alerts.

   o Additionally, AI tools can recognize previously unknown threats (i.e., zero-day attacks) by analyzing their behaviors rather than relying on pre-existing signatures.

3. **Threat Prediction**:

- By analyzing large datasets, machine learning algorithms can predict future attack vectors or patterns. For instance, ML can identify **emerging threats** by recognizing common patterns in attack strategies across different threat actors.

- These predictions allow threat hunters to proactively defend against potential threats rather than reacting to incidents after they have occurred.

Real-World Example: How an AI Tool Detected a New Variant of Malware That Had Previously Gone Unnoticed

A **tech company** was dealing with a persistent threat: an unknown variant of **malware** that had been evading traditional detection methods. The malware had previously gone undetected by their antivirus and endpoint protection tools.

- The organization integrated an **AI-based tool** designed to detect malware based on its behavior rather than relying on signature-based detection.

- The AI tool started by analyzing system processes, network traffic, and user behavior, and quickly identified an unusual pattern: an executable file was behaving in a way that was consistent with known malware but had never been seen before.

- **Findings**: The AI tool flagged the new variant of malware, which was then analyzed and contained before it could spread or cause damage.

- The integration of machine learning tools helped the company stay ahead of evolving threats, including those that were previously unseen by traditional security measures.

The techniques discussed in this chapter—**hypothesis-driven hunting**, **behavioral analysis**, and the use of **machine learning**—represent advanced methods for identifying and mitigating cyber threats. While traditional security measures often rely on static signatures or known attack patterns, these techniques allow threat hunters to approach security in a dynamic, proactive way, detecting even the most sophisticated attacks before they can cause significant harm.

Key Takeaways:

- **Hypothesis-Driven Hunting**: Start with a hypothesis based on threat intelligence or suspicious behavior, and use it to guide your investigation.

- **Behavioral Analysis**: Detect threats by studying abnormal behaviors and deviations from baseline activity rather than relying solely on known signatures.

- **Machine Learning**: Leverage AI and machine learning to automatically detect, classify, and predict threats, enabling faster and more accurate responses to attacks.

Chapter 8: Responding to Detected Threats

In this chapter, we will explore the **response** phase of threat hunting. Once a threat has been detected, it's crucial to act quickly and decisively to contain and mitigate the impact of the attack. A well-defined **incident response (IR) process** ensures that organizations can respond effectively to security breaches, reduce potential damage, and continuously improve their security posture.

Incident Response Process

The **Incident Response (IR) process** is a structured approach used by organizations to manage and mitigate the impact of a cybersecurity incident. Effective incident response requires preparedness, a defined strategy, and coordination among various stakeholders. The process generally consists of the following phases:

1. **Identification**:
   - This is the phase where the threat is first identified, typically by the threat-hunting team or automated detection tools. It's essential to have accurate identification to prevent false positives or delays in responding to actual threats.

2. **Containment**:

   o Containing the threat quickly is vital to stop it from spreading further into the network. This could involve isolating affected systems, blocking malicious IP addresses, or preventing the attacker from accessing critical resources.

3. **Eradication**:

   o Once the threat is contained, the focus shifts to eradicating the root cause. This could involve removing malware from infected systems, deleting compromised accounts, or patching vulnerabilities that were exploited during the attack.

4. **Recovery**:

   o After the threat is eradicated, the organization begins the process of recovery. This typically involves restoring data from backups, rebuilding systems, and ensuring that normal operations are resumed safely.

5. **Lessons Learned**:

   o The final step is the post-incident review, where the organization evaluates the effectiveness of its response. This is an opportunity to learn from the attack, improve security measures, and update the threat-hunting strategy.

Real-World Example: How Early Threat Hunting Led to Quick Containment of a Ransomware Attack

In a **large financial institution**, early detection of a ransomware attack helped the IT security team respond quickly and mitigate the damage.

- **Detection**: The organization's threat hunters had set up a continuous monitoring system to detect unusual file access patterns. They noticed that several systems began encrypting files unusually fast, which was a sign of ransomware activity.

- **Containment**: Upon identification, the threat-hunting team immediately isolated the infected systems from the network, preventing the ransomware from spreading to other critical systems. Additionally, they blocked outgoing communication with known malicious IP addresses that the ransomware was using to send encrypted data.

- **Eradication**: The compromised systems were thoroughly examined, and the ransomware was removed from all affected machines. The security team also identified the specific vulnerability that was exploited to gain access and patched it across the organization.

- **Recovery**: The organization restored encrypted files from backups, and systems were gradually brought back online in a secure manner.

- **Lessons Learned**: The incident prompted the company to implement additional security measures, including enhanced endpoint protection, better backup practices, and increased user training on phishing attacks, which were the primary vector for the ransomware.

This case demonstrates the importance of early threat detection, proactive response, and having an established incident response plan that can be quickly executed in a crisis.

Prioritizing Threats and Mitigation

Not all cybersecurity incidents are equal, and some threats require immediate attention due to their potential impact on the organization. **Prioritizing threats** is critical for ensuring that resources are allocated efficiently, and the most significant risks are addressed first.

Assessing the Severity of Threats and Deciding on Immediate Actions

1. **Severity Assessment**:
   - When a threat is detected, the **incident response team** must evaluate the severity and potential impact of the attack. Factors to consider include:
     - **Criticality of affected systems** (e.g., are financial systems or customer data involved?).
     - **Extent of the breach** (e.g., is the attack confined to one machine, or

has it spread across multiple systems?).

- **Potential for escalation** (e.g., is there evidence of an advanced persistent threat or lateral movement?).

2. **Mitigation**:

   o Once the severity has been assessed, the next step is to prioritize mitigation actions. For example, if the attack is deemed high-risk, the team may isolate affected systems immediately to prevent further damage, even if it means disrupting normal operations.

   o In other cases, mitigation might involve blocking suspicious network traffic or suspending user accounts that show signs of compromise.

3. **Communication**:

   o It's important to have clear communication during the response process, both internally (with other departments) and externally (with customers, stakeholders, and regulatory bodies if necessary).

Real-World Example: How Threat Hunters Mitigated a Sophisticated Attack by Isolating Affected Systems Immediately

A **global e-commerce company** faced a **sophisticated cyberattack** when threat actors attempted to exploit a **zero-day vulnerability** in their payment processing system.

- **Initial Detection**: A threat-hunting team monitoring network traffic noticed unusual behavior—large volumes of data were being transmitted from an internal server to an unknown IP address.

- **Assessment**: The team immediately assessed the severity of the situation. Given the volume of data being exfiltrated and the nature of the affected system (critical for payment processing), they determined that the attack was likely in its early stages but posed a high risk.

- **Mitigation**: The team prioritized containing the threat by immediately isolating the affected systems, including the server in question, from the network. This quick action prevented the attackers from obtaining sensitive customer payment data.

- **Root Cause**: The attackers had exploited a **zero-day vulnerability** in the payment application, which was patched immediately after containment.

- **Outcome**: The attack was successfully mitigated without significant financial loss, and the company initiated further investigations to strengthen their defenses.

This example highlights the importance of rapid response and effective containment strategies when dealing with sophisticated attacks. Swift action by the threat-hunting team helped limit the scope of the attack and protected sensitive customer data.

Post-Incident Analysis and Improvement

After a cybersecurity incident, it's crucial to conduct a **post-mortem** to analyze the attack, assess the effectiveness of the response, and identify areas for improvement. The goal of post-incident analysis is to learn from each event and continuously enhance the organization's ability to detect and respond to future threats.

Reviewing the Attack Post-Mortem to Improve Defenses and Hunting Tactics

1. **Incident Review**:

   o   After the dust settles, the team should perform a thorough **review of the incident**, looking at each phase of the incident response process: identification, containment, eradication, and recovery.

   o   This review should identify what went well, what challenges arose, and how different tools, processes, or personnel could have been more effective.

2. **Identifying Gaps**:

   o   A **post-incident analysis** should also highlight any gaps in the organization's security posture or response plan. For example, if the attack was detected late, it may indicate that monitoring systems need to be improved or that threat-hunting efforts need to be expanded.

3. **Implementing Improvements**:

   o Based on the post-mortem findings, the organization can implement new procedures, update tools, and improve training to prepare for future incidents. This might include enhancing detection capabilities, updating response protocols, or even strengthening employee awareness training.

Real-World Example: How Lessons from a Previous Attack Led to Faster Detection and Prevention of Future Threats

A **large healthcare provider** suffered a **data breach** when attackers gained access to its internal network through a compromised employee account. After the breach was contained, the company conducted a **post-incident analysis** to identify lessons learned.

- **Root Cause**: The breach occurred because the company's password policies were not strict enough, and multi-factor authentication (MFA) was not in place.

- **Improvements**: Based on the analysis, the healthcare provider decided to:

   o **Implement stricter password policies** (e.g., mandatory use of complex passwords and frequent changes).

- o **Introduce multi-factor authentication** for all employees, especially for those accessing sensitive healthcare data.

- o **Enhance monitoring** by integrating **behavioral analysis** into the threat-hunting process to detect suspicious login attempts and unauthorized access patterns.

- **Outcome**: In the months following these changes, the organization successfully detected and mitigated a similar attack before it could escalate, significantly improving their ability to respond to threats and preventing future data breaches.

In this chapter, we've covered the **incident response process, prioritizing threats and mitigation**, and **post-incident analysis and improvement**. Threat hunters don't just detect and mitigate threats—they also play a crucial role in ensuring the organization learns from each incident, strengthens its defenses, and improves its overall security posture.

Key Takeaways:

- A **structured incident response process** is essential for effective threat containment and recovery.

- **Prioritizing threats** based on severity helps allocate resources efficiently and minimize damage.

- **Post-incident analysis** is vital for identifying security gaps and improving defenses for future attacks.

These processes are the backbone of a resilient cybersecurity strategy, helping organizations stay ahead of evolving threats.

Chapter 9: False Positives and Tuning Your Threat Hunting Efforts

In the world of threat hunting, **false positives** are one of the biggest challenges. They can overwhelm security teams, distract from real threats, and waste valuable time and resources. However, by fine-tuning threat-hunting tools and techniques, organizations can reduce false positives, improve detection accuracy, and optimize their hunting efforts. This chapter will dive into how to deal with false positives, tune your tools for better performance, and continuously refine your threat-hunting strategy.

Dealing with False Positives

False positives in threat hunting refer to legitimate activities that are flagged as suspicious or malicious. These false alarms can lead to unnecessary investigations and responses, which can distract threat hunters from more critical issues. While it's important to avoid missing a real threat, it's equally important not to waste resources chasing false positives.

Techniques for Reducing False Positives:

1. **Filtering Noise**:

    o   **Noise** refers to a large volume of harmless or routine activities that can clutter the data and make it harder to spot real threats. Reducing noise helps improve focus and efficiency. Threat hunters use **data filtering** techniques to exclude non-threatening activities or to focus on certain types of incidents that are more likely to indicate an attack.

    o   Example: If a certain type of traffic is common in the network but isn't malicious, it can be filtered out to focus on more relevant activities.

2. **Adjusting Detection Thresholds**:

    o   Threat-hunting tools often operate based on certain thresholds—if an activity exceeds a set threshold, it triggers an alert. For instance, if a user downloads a large number of files or makes an unusually large number of failed login attempts, it could trigger an alert.

    o   **Tuning** these thresholds is important to ensure they are not set too low (causing too many alerts) or too high (risking missing real threats). Fine-tuning the threshold can strike a balance between sensitivity and specificity.

3. **Contextual Awareness**:

- Understanding the environment and context of the data helps in distinguishing between real threats and benign activity. For instance, an unusual login might be a threat if it comes from an unrecognized location, but if it's from an employee on business travel, it may be legitimate.

- **Contextual awareness** involves considering factors like time of day, the user's behavior, and known patterns within the organization to determine if an alert is worth investigating.

Real-World Example: How False Positives Were Reduced by Fine-Tuning an EDR Tool

In one case, a **large e-commerce company** was using an **Endpoint Detection and Response (EDR)** tool to monitor network activity and detect possible malware infections. Initially, the EDR system was generating a large number of false positives, particularly around employee activities like accessing several files in quick succession during busy shopping seasons.

- **Problem**: The EDR tool was flagging the behavior as suspicious, generating unnecessary alerts. These false positives slowed down the team's ability to investigate real threats.

- **Solution**: The security team decided to fine-tune the EDR tool by adjusting its **behavioral baselines** and setting thresholds for **file access patterns**. They set up rules that accounted for high traffic during peak hours, such as Black Friday, and allowed for quick processing of legitimate user activity.

- **Outcome**: By adjusting the tool's thresholds and creating more realistic baselines, the team was able to reduce false positives by 40%, allowing the hunters to focus more on potential real threats.

Tuning and Optimizing Threat Hunting Tools

No matter how advanced your tools are, they need to be **tuned and optimized** to your organization's specific environment. Tools like **SIEM (Security Information and Event Management)**, **EDR (Endpoint Detection and Response)**, and other monitoring solutions must be configured to reflect your network's behavior, user patterns, and typical attack methods. Optimizing these tools ensures that threat hunting becomes more efficient and accurate over time.

Improving the Effectiveness of Tools like SIEM by Tuning Them Based on Specific Network Behaviors

1. **Behavioral Tuning**:
   - SIEM tools collect and analyze log data from multiple sources (firewalls, endpoints, servers, etc.). By analyzing this data, threat hunters can detect abnormal activity that may signal a threat. **Tuning** SIEM tools based on your network's specific **traffic patterns**, business hours, and communication protocols helps to narrow down what is abnormal and what is normal.

o For example, if your company's employees typically access cloud resources in the afternoon, but SIEM detects a surge in activity at 3 AM, that could be a sign of malicious activity, such as a brute-force attack.

2. **Customizing Alerts**:

   o Standard detection rules might not work well for every organization. By customizing the alerting system, you can filter out known benign activities and focus on more complex threats that warrant attention. This could involve tuning the **risk scoring** or **alert thresholds** based on the type of data being monitored.

3. **Integration of Threat Intelligence**:

   o One way to improve the effectiveness of tools like SIEM is to integrate them with **threat intelligence platforms**. Threat intelligence provides valuable information about emerging attack vectors, tactics, techniques, and procedures (TTPs). By configuring SIEM tools to correlate known TTPs with incoming data, threat hunters can detect novel attacks earlier.

Real-World Example: How a Security Team Used Better Filtering to Focus on Real Threats

In a **mid-sized healthcare provider**, a security team using a SIEM tool struggled to differentiate between legitimate traffic and real threats. Their SIEM was generating a large number of alerts from users accessing health records outside of business hours.

- **Problem**: The SIEM was overwhelmed by repetitive alerts, particularly from employees working late or from departments with irregular hours. The team was spending too much time chasing down minor incidents, which was distracting them from critical threats.

- **Solution**: The team decided to **fine-tune** their SIEM tool to include more **contextual data**. They adjusted the **time-based thresholds** to allow more flexibility for legitimate access, integrated additional **role-based access control** (RBAC) data, and configured the SIEM to focus on more **complex attack patterns**.

- **Outcome**: After optimizing the SIEM tool, the team reduced the volume of alerts by 50% and improved the accuracy of threat detection. Real threats were more easily identified, and the time to respond to incidents was reduced significantly.

Continuous Refinement and Feedback

Threat hunting is not a one-time process—it's iterative. As new threats emerge, hunting techniques must evolve. A successful threat-hunting program embraces **continuous refinement** and feedback loops to ensure that it is always improving and adapting to the changing threat landscape.

The Iterative Nature of Threat Hunting: Learn, Adapt, Improve

1. **Feedback Loop**:

   o Threat hunting is a continuous cycle that involves learning from each investigation, adapting techniques, and improving the tools used for detection. Each new threat or false alarm presents an opportunity to refine the hunting process.

2. **Lessons Learned**:

   o After each hunt or detected threat, a **post-hunt analysis** should be conducted. This helps identify what went well, what didn't, and where improvements can be made. Are there new types of threats that need more attention? Did you miss any indicators that could have helped detect the threat earlier?

3. **Continuous Training**:

   o As technology evolves, so do the skills required for effective threat hunting. Regular training and skill development are essential for staying up to date with new techniques, tools, and attack methods.

Real-World Example: How Ongoing Feedback Helped Improve a Company's Threat-Hunting Program Over Time

A **telecom company** initially started with a basic threat-hunting program that was heavily reliant on traditional detection tools. However, they quickly realized that while their SIEM tool could catch simple threats, it was missing advanced ones like **advanced persistent threats (APTs)** or **lateral movement**.

- **Early Struggles**: The initial alerts were overwhelming, and the team had difficulty prioritizing them. They lacked a strategy for filtering out the noise and focusing on the most critical threats.

- **Solution**: After gathering feedback from their team and analyzing the types of threats they were missing, they began to adopt a more structured hunting process, integrating **behavioral analysis** and **machine learning** into their strategy.

- **Outcome**: Over time, their threat-hunting program became more effective. Feedback from analysts and the lessons learned from each hunt allowed the company to fine-tune their approach and improve detection accuracy. This iterative process led to **faster identification of APTs**, reduced response time, and better overall protection against emerging threats.

This chapter has focused on the critical aspects of dealing with **false positives** and **tuning your threat-hunting efforts**. Here are the key takeaways:

- **False positives** can be reduced through **noise filtering**, **adjusting detection thresholds**, and **contextual awareness**.

- **Tuning threat-hunting tools** like SIEM and EDR improves detection efficiency and helps focus on real threats.

- **Continuous refinement and feedback** are essential for the iterative improvement of threat-hunting programs, ensuring they evolve with the changing threat landscape.

Effective threat hunting requires not only the right tools and techniques but also an ongoing commitment to refinement and adaptation. By incorporating feedback, learning from each incident, and tuning detection systems, organizations can significantly enhance their ability to detect and respond to threats.

Chapter 10: Threat Intelligence and Its Role in Threat Hunting

In the evolving world of cybersecurity, **threat intelligence** plays an indispensable role in **threat hunting**. By leveraging actionable information about potential threats, threat hunters can proactively search for and neutralize adversaries before they cause significant damage. This chapter explores the vital role of threat intelligence in enhancing threat-hunting efforts, how to integrate it into the hunting process, and the value of collaboration across industries to improve overall security.

What is Threat Intelligence?

Threat intelligence refers to the collection and analysis of information regarding current and potential cyber threats. It involves understanding the tactics, techniques, and procedures (TTPs) that threat actors use to infiltrate and compromise systems. This information can come from a variety of sources, including open-source intelligence (OSINT), government agencies, threat intelligence platforms, commercial providers, and even the data shared among organizations.

Definition and Importance of Threat Intelligence in Threat Hunting:

- **Definition**: Threat intelligence is the knowledge of existing or emerging threats to an organization's assets, including the identity and motives of threat actors, their attack methods, and indicators of compromise (IOCs) like IP addresses, domain names, and file hashes.

- **Importance**:

  - **Proactive Defense**: Threat intelligence allows threat hunters to be proactive by giving them detailed information about the latest attack trends and vulnerabilities that they can search for within their network.

  - **Informed Hypotheses**: It helps threat hunters form well-grounded hypotheses about potential attack vectors, guiding their search efforts in more focused and efficient ways.

  - **Enhanced Detection**: By continuously updating their tools with the latest intelligence, organizations can ensure that they are capable of detecting emerging threats faster, even before specific signatures or known attack patterns are fully identified.

Real-World Example: How Using Threat Intelligence Feeds Helped a Company Detect a Zero-Day Attack

A **financial institution** had integrated **threat intelligence feeds** into its Security Information and Event Management (SIEM) system. The organization had a policy of regularly updating its defenses with fresh threat intelligence, including real-time alerts about emerging vulnerabilities.

- **Problem**: One day, threat intelligence feeds revealed a **zero-day vulnerability** in a popular web server software being used by the institution. The threat intelligence feed included IOCs tied to a specific malware variant exploiting this vulnerability.

- **Solution**: The security team quickly implemented additional defenses based on the threat intelligence, including **patching the vulnerable software**, blocking known malicious IP addresses, and deploying new detection rules to monitor for signs of the attack.

- **Outcome**: Thanks to the timely intelligence, the financial institution was able to prevent the exploit from taking place, safeguarding its critical infrastructure and sensitive customer data.

Integrating Threat Intelligence into Hunting

Threat intelligence is a cornerstone of an effective threat-hunting strategy. When integrated properly, it helps sharpen the focus of hunting efforts, providing relevant data and context that guide hunters to the right places in the network.

Using Threat Intelligence to Fuel Hypotheses and Inform Hunting:

1. **Forming Hypotheses**:

    o   Threat intelligence enables hunters to craft more precise and informed hypotheses. By knowing what tactics, techniques, and procedures (TTPs) adversaries are using, hunters can hypothesize where the attackers might be operating in the network, what they might be trying to achieve, and how to detect their activity.

    o   Example: If the threat intelligence reports that a specific APT group is targeting organizations using outdated VPN software, a threat hunter might hypothesize that they will find traces of compromised VPN connections in the organization's network logs.

2. **Focused Data Collection**:

    o   Once a hypothesis is formed, threat intelligence can guide the collection of relevant data. This means focusing on particular **logs, endpoints, or network traffic patterns** that align with the known attack methods or indicators shared in the threat intelligence feed.

3. **Enhancing Detection Rules**:

    o   Threat intelligence can be used to create or refine detection rules within security tools like SIEM, firewalls, or IDS/IPS systems. For example, if new **malware hashes** are included in the intelligence, they can be added to the detection system to monitor for potential intrusions.

Real-World Example: How Threat Intelligence from an External Provider Alerted a Company to a New Attack Technique

A **large manufacturing company** had subscribed to an external threat intelligence provider that monitored advanced persistent threats (APTs). The provider issued a warning that a new **fileless malware** technique was being used to attack organizations in their industry.

- **Problem**: The company had not yet updated its threat-hunting strategy to account for the possibility of fileless malware, which doesn't leave traditional file-based traces and can evade many detection methods.

- **Solution**: The threat intelligence provider shared detailed information about the new attack technique, including how attackers were executing commands directly in memory, making it difficult to detect with signature-based tools. The company integrated this information into its **endpoint detection and response (EDR)** system and updated its detection rules to flag suspicious in-memory processes.

- **Outcome**: A few weeks later, the company detected an ongoing **fileless malware attack** targeting its network. By using the provided intelligence, the threat hunters were able to identify and contain the attack before any damage was done.

Sharing Intelligence for Collaborative Hunting

Cyber threats are increasingly complex and can often span multiple organizations, industries, and even countries. This has led to an increasing emphasis on **information sharing** to improve overall detection and response capabilities across the cybersecurity community.

The Role of Information Sharing in Improving Threat Detection Across Industries:

1. **Collaborative Detection**:

    o   By sharing threat intelligence, organizations can benefit from the collective knowledge of a broader network of security professionals. Collaboration helps to identify trends, discover new attack techniques, and rapidly disseminate IOCs to others in the industry.

    o   For example, financial institutions might share information about a new type of fraud attack that's targeting banks or credit unions.

2. **Better Preparedness**:

    o   Industry-specific organizations or sector-specific Information Sharing and Analysis Centers (ISACs) facilitate this exchange. These centers promote collaboration by helping businesses within the same sector share threat intelligence securely.

- o This collaboration allows for faster detection of attacks, better preparation for emerging threats, and more robust response strategies across multiple organizations.

3. **Threat Intelligence Platforms**:

   - o Some organizations use **Threat Intelligence Platforms (TIPs)** to centralize and automate the sharing of threat intelligence. These platforms allow organizations to aggregate intelligence from multiple sources, correlate it, and distribute it in a format that is easily actionable by threat hunters.

Real-World Example: How a Group of Organizations Shared Threat Intelligence to Thwart an Ongoing Attack

In 2020, a **large multinational corporation** and a **group of smaller companies** in the healthcare sector were targeted by a sophisticated cybercriminal gang known for **ransomware attacks**. Initially, only one of the organizations detected unusual activity, but upon sharing their findings through an **ISAC**, the other companies quickly realized they had been targeted as well.

- **Problem**: The threat actors were using advanced **lateral movement techniques** to infiltrate multiple systems, and the attack was spreading rapidly.

- **Solution**: Once the organizations shared threat intelligence (including IOCs, attack techniques, and affected systems), they were able to cross-reference their findings, identify common vulnerabilities, and implement emergency mitigation steps. They also coordinated responses to isolate the attack and prevent further infiltration.

- **Outcome**: The collaborative sharing of intelligence allowed the group to identify the attack early in its lifecycle, implement defensive measures across their networks, and prevent a full-scale ransomware outbreak. The timely exchange of information played a key role in minimizing damage and ensuring business continuity.

In this chapter, we have seen how **threat intelligence** significantly enhances the **threat-hunting process** by providing critical, actionable information. The key points covered include:

- **What Threat Intelligence Is**: It involves knowledge of the current and emerging threats, which helps hunters anticipate potential attack vectors and strengthen defenses.

- **Integrating Threat Intelligence**: By using intelligence to inform hypotheses, guide data collection, and optimize detection rules, threat hunters can be much more focused and effective.

- **Collaborative Information Sharing**: Threat intelligence sharing across organizations and industries helps to identify trends, improve preparedness, and enhance collective defense against common adversaries.

Threat intelligence is not only about gathering information but about making that information actionable and relevant to an organization's specific threat-hunting needs. When used correctly, it empowers security teams to stay ahead of cybercriminals and protect their organizations more effectively.

Chapter 11: Threat Hunting in Different Environments

As organizations expand their digital infrastructure, the environments they operate in become increasingly diverse. This chapter explores how threat hunting adapts to various environments, including the cloud, hybrid networks, on-premise systems, and the Internet of Things (IoT). Each environment presents unique challenges and opportunities for threat hunters to leverage their tools, methodologies, and intelligence in different ways. We will discuss the particular nuances of each environment and provide real-world examples to illustrate how threat hunters have successfully detected and mitigated threats in these varied settings.

Threat Hunting in the Cloud

The rise of cloud computing has drastically changed the way organizations deploy and manage their IT infrastructure. Public cloud services like **AWS**, **Microsoft Azure**, and **Google Cloud** provide scalability and flexibility, but they also introduce new security challenges. Threat hunting in the cloud differs from traditional on-premise environments due to the shared responsibility model, dynamic nature of cloud resources, and the complexity of cloud-native technologies.

Cloud Threat Hunting:

- **Shared Responsibility Model**: Cloud providers are responsible for securing the infrastructure, while customers are responsible for securing their applications, data, and access management. Threat hunters must focus on monitoring the customer's side of the stack (such as user activity, configurations, and data flows) while also leveraging any cloud-native security tools.

- **Dynamic Environments**: Cloud environments are highly dynamic, with resources constantly being spun up and down. This requires threat hunters to continuously monitor for abnormal activity and misconfigurations that could introduce vulnerabilities, such as improperly secured cloud storage buckets or unauthorized access to cloud APIs.

- **Tool Integration**: Tools that integrate seamlessly with cloud platforms, like **AWS CloudTrail**, **Azure Security Center**, or **Google Cloud Security Command Center**, are essential for gathering logs and detecting suspicious activity.

Real-World Example: How a Cloud Provider Helped Identify and Block a DDoS Attack in Real-Time

In 2021, a **large e-commerce platform** that hosted its infrastructure in AWS was targeted by a **Distributed Denial-of-Service (DDoS) attack**. The platform had integrated **AWS Shield** and **AWS WAF (Web Application Firewall)**, which are cloud-native tools designed to detect and mitigate DDoS threats in real-time.

- **Problem**: The attackers launched a high-volume DDoS attack designed to overwhelm the platform's servers and disrupt service for its users.

- **Solution**: Thanks to the cloud-based threat-hunting tools, AWS was able to quickly detect the abnormal traffic patterns and alert the e-commerce platform's security team. AWS Shield automatically mitigated the attack by redirecting the traffic to DDoS mitigation servers, filtering out malicious traffic.

- **Outcome**: The DDoS attack was blocked without any service disruption, demonstrating the importance of having cloud-native tools and threat-hunting processes integrated with the cloud provider's security offerings.

Threat Hunting in Hybrid and On-Premise Networks

In contrast to cloud environments, **hybrid IT environments** combine both cloud and on-premise infrastructure, often creating complexities in terms of visibility, monitoring, and response. Organizations that operate in hybrid environments need to coordinate their threat-hunting efforts across both types of infrastructure while ensuring that security is maintained throughout.

Challenges in Hybrid Environments:

- **Disparate Systems**: Cloud and on-premise networks often use different tools and technologies for security monitoring, making it difficult to consolidate data and apply consistent security measures.

- **Data Flow and Network Visibility**: It can be harder to track data flow between on-premise systems and cloud environments, creating potential gaps in visibility and allowing threats to go undetected.

- **Security Tools Integration**: Ensuring that on-premise tools, like SIEM systems and firewalls, work seamlessly with cloud-native solutions is crucial for an effective threat-hunting strategy.

Real-World Example: How a Hybrid Network Led to Complexities in Detection but Was Mitigated with Cross-Platform Tools

A **financial services company** operated both on-premise infrastructure and cloud-based services across AWS and Azure. One day, the company noticed unusual activity in its cloud environment, with a large number of failed login attempts on cloud servers. However, the company's on-premise security team was unable to correlate this with any activity happening within their internal network.

- **Problem**: The security team found that while the cloud environment was showing signs of compromise, they lacked the necessary visibility into the interactions between their on-premise network and the cloud, which led to confusion about whether the attack was part of a larger, coordinated breach.

- **Solution**: By implementing a **cross-platform threat-hunting tool** that could integrate with both cloud services and on-premise systems, the team gained better visibility into how the attackers were moving between environments. Using a **cloud SIEM** system that was connected to their on-premise **security appliances**, the team correlated data from failed login attempts and suspicious network traffic to identify an ongoing attack.

- **Outcome**: The financial services company was able to successfully identify and block the attacker's movement from the cloud into their internal network, preventing a breach and protecting sensitive data across both environments.

IoT Security and Threat Hunting

The growing number of **Internet of Things (IoT)** devices introduces unique vulnerabilities to organizations. IoT devices, such as smart sensors, cameras, industrial control systems, and medical devices, often lack robust security features, making them attractive targets for attackers. As more IoT devices are connected to both enterprise networks and the broader internet, their potential to be exploited for cyberattacks grows.

Emerging Threats in IoT Devices:

- **Insecure Devices**: Many IoT devices are designed for convenience rather than security, often lacking encryption, authentication, or regular software updates.

- **Botnets**: IoT devices can be compromised and used as part of a **botnet** to launch attacks such as DDoS or to spread malware across networks.

- **Lack of Visibility**: IoT devices may be on networks without proper monitoring, and their activity often goes undetected unless specific threat-hunting efforts are made to identify them.

The Need for Dedicated Threat-Hunting Efforts:

- IoT devices introduce a layer of complexity to an organization's security posture. Security teams need specialized threat-hunting methods and tools to identify abnormal behavior in these devices.

- Because many IoT devices are not built with security in mind, it is essential for organizations to incorporate dedicated **IoT security monitoring** tools that can monitor network traffic, device behaviors, and any potential vulnerabilities in these devices.

Real-World Example: How a Smart Device Vulnerability Led to the Discovery of a Wider Attack on an Industrial Control System

A **manufacturing company** that used an **Industrial Control System (ICS)** for managing production was targeted by cybercriminals exploiting vulnerabilities in connected **smart thermostats** used to regulate the factory's temperature. The threat hunters were able to identify unusual network traffic coming from one of the smart thermostats, which had been compromised.

- **Problem**: The thermostat was part of the IoT ecosystem used in the factory, and its network behavior seemed benign at first. However, a **threat hunter** noticed an anomaly—data was being sent to an external IP address that had previously been identified as a **command-and-control server** for a botnet.

- **Solution**: Upon investigating further, the security team realized that the attackers had gained access to the thermostat, used it as a foothold, and then moved laterally through the factory's ICS network. The team quickly isolated the device and contained the threat before it could spread further.

- **Outcome**: The breach was contained and the security team implemented additional monitoring tools specifically designed for IoT devices, enabling them to detect similar anomalies in the future.

In this chapter, we explored how **threat hunting** adapts to different environments—**cloud, hybrid networks, on-premise systems**, and **IoT devices**—each of which presents unique challenges and requires tailored strategies. The key points covered include:

- **Threat Hunting in the Cloud**: Leveraging cloud-native security tools and understanding the shared responsibility model are essential for effective cloud threat hunting.

- **Threat Hunting in Hybrid and On-Premise Networks**: Managing complex, cross-platform security tools and data flows across hybrid environments is crucial for detecting threats across both cloud and on-premise assets.

- **IoT Security and Threat Hunting**: The rapid growth of IoT devices demands specialized tools and methods to detect abnormal behaviors and mitigate risks associated with these inherently insecure devices.

As organizations continue to adopt new technologies and architectures, threat hunting must evolve to meet the demands of these ever-changing environments. By understanding the unique challenges and using the right tools, threat hunters can enhance their organization's ability to detect, respond to, and mitigate threats in the cloud, on-premise networks, and the IoT landscape.

Chapter 12: The Legal and Ethical Aspects of Threat Hunting

While threat hunting is essential for identifying and mitigating cyber threats, it comes with a set of legal and ethical responsibilities that must be understood and adhered to. As the cybersecurity landscape evolves, so too does the regulatory environment. This chapter discusses the legal boundaries of threat hunting, the ethical considerations that must be taken into account, and the role of law enforcement in handling cybercrime. By understanding these aspects, threat hunters can ensure they are operating within the law and maintaining ethical standards while protecting their organizations.

Legal Boundaries in Threat Hunting

As threat hunters gain access to sensitive systems, logs, and data during their investigations, they must be aware of the legal frameworks governing privacy and data protection. Several regulations, including **General Data Protection Regulation (GDPR)** and the **California Consumer Privacy Act (CCPA)**, have been enacted to ensure that organizations handle personal data with care and respect.

Key Legal Considerations in Threat Hunting:

- **Data Privacy Regulations**: GDPR and CCPA are two of the most well-known regulations that impact the way threat hunters conduct investigations. GDPR requires organizations to follow strict rules when handling personal data, including ensuring that personal data is only collected for lawful purposes and that data subjects are notified of any data collection. Similarly, the CCPA gives California residents the right to access, delete, and opt-out of the sale of their personal data.

- **Scope of Access**: Threat hunters need to ensure that their activities are limited to the scope of what is legally permitted. For instance, accessing private email communications or personal files without explicit consent can lead to violations of privacy laws.

- **Chain of Custody**: Threat hunters must maintain a secure and documented chain of custody for evidence gathered during investigations. Improper handling of evidence—such as altering logs or storing data improperly—can render the evidence inadmissible in court and create potential legal challenges.

Real-World Example: How Improper Handling of Data During an Investigation Led to Compliance Issues

In a **high-profile case involving a financial institution**, a threat hunting team discovered evidence of a potential data breach involving customer data. However, during the investigation, the team accessed several internal systems containing sensitive financial and personal information, which they were not authorized to examine under the company's internal policies and applicable regulations.

- **Problem**: Although the investigators had the best intentions of uncovering a potential breach, their actions violated GDPR by accessing personal data without proper consent or a valid legal basis. The data was not handled according to the institution's privacy guidelines, which exposed the organization to significant fines and reputational damage.

- **Solution**: After the breach was discovered, the organization had to report the incident to relevant authorities and immediately implement corrective actions to strengthen its internal data handling policies. The incident resulted in fines, but it also prompted a review of the company's threat-hunting policies and better training for staff on compliance with privacy regulations.

- **Outcome**: The company put in place stricter protocols for how threat-hunting teams interact with data, ensuring compliance with all relevant privacy regulations. This case highlighted the importance of balancing security efforts with legal requirements in threat hunting.

Ethical Considerations in Threat Hunting

Ethics plays a critical role in threat hunting, as hunters often have access to sensitive personal and organizational data during their investigations. Ethical dilemmas can arise when personal information, employee communications, or other sensitive data is involved. Threat hunters must make decisions that balance the need for security with respect for privacy and the rights of individuals.

Key Ethical Considerations:

- **Respecting Privacy**: Even when conducting threat hunting activities, it is crucial to respect the privacy of individuals. This means ensuring that any sensitive or personal data discovered during investigations is handled with care and only used for legitimate purposes related to the security investigation.

- **Minimizing Intrusiveness**: Threat hunters should always aim to minimize their intrusion into the personal or organizational data they are examining. For example, if a threat hunter is analyzing network traffic, they should focus on identifying threats rather than examining the content of communications unless absolutely necessary for the investigation.

- **Transparency**: Ethical threat hunters should be transparent about their activities, keeping appropriate stakeholders informed of the scope and methods used during investigations. This transparency helps build trust within the organization and ensures that employees and customers understand how their data is being handled.

Real-World Example: How Ethical Concerns Influenced How Data Was Handled During a Corporate Breach Investigation

A **multinational retail corporation** experienced a data breach involving customer payment card information. During the investigation, the security team gained access to the internal systems where payment data was stored, along with other personal details about customers.

- **Problem**: The investigation raised ethical concerns, as the team had to ensure that no unnecessary personal data was accessed or retained. For example, although they were focused on finding the breach, the team had to ensure they did not inadvertently expose additional customer information during the investigation.

- **Solution**: The company implemented strict ethical guidelines for handling customer data during the breach investigation. Only the minimum amount of data necessary for detecting the breach was accessed, and all personally identifiable information was anonymized or encrypted whenever possible.

- **Outcome**: The ethical handling of customer data helped the organization maintain its reputation and trust with customers. The incident also reinforced the importance of having a robust ethical framework for cybersecurity investigations, ensuring that security measures do not infringe upon privacy rights.

Cooperation with Law Enforcement

In certain cases, threat hunters may uncover evidence of cybercriminal activity that requires the involvement of law enforcement. Cooperation with law enforcement agencies is essential to ensure that perpetrators are held accountable, and that any criminal activity is properly investigated and prosecuted. Threat hunters must understand how to work within the legal framework when escalating an issue to law enforcement.

Key Aspects of Cooperation:

- **Reporting to Authorities**: When threat hunters uncover evidence of a serious crime, such as data theft or ransomware attacks, they must notify the relevant authorities. Depending on the jurisdiction, there may be legal requirements for reporting certain types of incidents within a specific time frame.

- **Sharing Threat Intelligence**: Threat intelligence is valuable not only for improving an organization's security posture but also for assisting law enforcement in tracking down cybercriminals. Sharing anonymized threat intelligence with law enforcement or industry groups can help build a larger picture of cybercriminal activity.

- **Preserving Evidence**: When working with law enforcement, it is critical to ensure that all evidence collected during the investigation is preserved in a way that maintains its integrity. This includes following proper chain-of-custody protocols and ensuring that all data is admissible in court if needed.

Real-World Example: How a Company Worked with Authorities to Track Down a Cybercriminal

In 2020, a **global technology firm** was the victim of a sophisticated cyberattack involving a ransomware group that had encrypted the company's critical data and demanded a large ransom. After conducting an internal investigation, the company discovered the ransomware attack was part of a larger coordinated cybercriminal campaign.

- **Problem**: The company was unsure of how to proceed. While they had isolated the ransomware, they knew that the perpetrators had likely targeted other organizations as well.

- **Solution**: The company cooperated with **national cybersecurity authorities**, including law enforcement agencies and CERTs (Computer Emergency Response Teams), sharing key indicators of compromise (IOCs) and detailed forensic evidence from their systems. They also provided information about the ransomware's origins, including the group's tactics, techniques, and procedures (TTPs).

- **Outcome**: The collaboration between the company and law enforcement led to the identification and arrest of several individuals behind the ransomware attacks. This case demonstrated how private organizations can work together with authorities to address and combat cybercrime on a larger scale.

In this chapter, we explored the **legal and ethical aspects of threat hunting**, focusing on the responsibilities threat hunters must adhere to when conducting investigations. The key topics covered included:

- **Legal Boundaries**: Understanding data privacy laws, the scope of access, and maintaining chain of custody is essential to avoid legal pitfalls during threat-hunting activities.

- **Ethical Considerations**: Threat hunters must balance security with privacy and transparency, ensuring that their activities do not violate ethical standards or infringe upon individual rights.

- **Cooperation with Law Enforcement**: In cases of cybercrime, threat hunters must know when and how to involve law enforcement, ensuring evidence is preserved and threat intelligence is shared appropriately.

By respecting these legal and ethical guidelines, threat hunters can conduct their work more effectively while building trust with stakeholders and ensuring that investigations are conducted in a responsible and lawful manner.

Chapter 13: Building a Career in Threat Hunting

Cybersecurity is a dynamic and ever-growing field, with an increasing demand for skilled professionals capable of identifying and mitigating advanced threats. Among these professionals, **threat hunters** play a crucial role in proactively seeking out vulnerabilities and threats that bypass traditional security measures. But how does one get started in this exciting and challenging career path? This chapter outlines the skills and qualifications needed to become a successful threat hunter, career pathways within the cybersecurity field, and provides a practical guide for beginners to begin their journey in threat hunting.

Skills and Qualifications

To become a successful threat hunter, one must possess a unique set of skills and qualifications. These go beyond basic knowledge of cybersecurity and require a deep understanding of how attacks are carried out, how systems and networks function, and how to analyze and interpret security data.

Key Skills for Threat Hunting:

1. **Analytical Thinking**: Threat hunters need to be able to think critically and methodically. They must be able to analyze large volumes of data, identify patterns, and recognize anomalous behavior that could signal a cyber threat.

2. **Networking Knowledge**: A strong understanding of networking protocols, IP addresses, firewalls, routers, and switches is essential for threat hunters. The ability to trace data flow across networks and detect unusual activities is fundamental to threat detection.

3. **Familiarity with Operating Systems**: Threat hunters need to understand the internals of both operating systems (Windows, Linux, macOS) and the common services they run. This knowledge is critical when investigating compromised systems.

4. **Proficiency with Security Tools**: Threat hunters need hands-on experience with a range of security tools, such as **SIEM (Security Information and Event Management)** systems, **EDR (Endpoint Detection and Response)** tools, and threat intelligence platforms. Experience with malware analysis tools and network traffic analysis is also beneficial.

5. **Scripting and Automation**: Automation is key to effective threat hunting. Understanding scripting languages like Python or PowerShell allows hunters to automate repetitive tasks and build custom tools for specific investigations.

6. **Incident Response Knowledge**: Threat hunters often work closely with incident response teams.

Knowledge of incident response procedures, containment strategies, and remediation processes is critical.

Certifications for Threat Hunting:

Certain certifications can greatly enhance a candidate's qualifications and credibility in the field of threat hunting. Some key certifications include:

- **Certified Information Systems Security Professional (CISSP)**: A widely recognized certification in cybersecurity.

- **Certified Ethical Hacker (CEH)**: Focuses on penetration testing and ethical hacking techniques.

- **GIAC Cyber Threat Intelligence (GCTI)**: Specializes in understanding and responding to cyber threats.

- **Certified Threat Intelligence Analyst (CTIA)**: Aimed at professionals who analyze threat intelligence data.

- **CompTIA Security+**: Provides foundational knowledge for security professionals, including threat detection.

Real-World Example: Profiles of Successful Threat Hunters

A good example of a successful threat hunter is **Jane Doe**, who started as a network administrator before transitioning into cybersecurity. Jane spent years working with security systems and quickly developed an interest in threat detection. She earned certifications in **CISSP** and **CEH**, which led to a role as a security analyst at a large financial institution. After honing her skills in malware analysis and intrusion detection, she was promoted to a lead threat hunter position. Today, she leads a team of hunters who proactively detect and mitigate threats before they cause damage.

Career Pathways in Cybersecurity

Cybersecurity offers various career pathways, and threat hunting is one of the most specialized and rewarding roles in the field. As you advance in your career, there are several options for growth, depending on your interests and skillset.

Key Roles in Cybersecurity:

1. **Security Analyst**: Often an entry-level position, security analysts monitor security systems, detect vulnerabilities, and assist in incident response. It is a great entry point for those interested in threat hunting.

2. **Threat Hunter**: After gaining some experience in security analysis, many professionals transition into threat hunting. Threat hunters take a more proactive role, scanning for hidden threats that may bypass traditional security measures.

3. **Incident Responder**: While threat hunters focus on detection, incident responders are experts in managing and containing security incidents once they have been identified. A role in incident

response can be an excellent complement to threat hunting experience.

4. **Security Architect**: Security architects design and build systems and networks with security in mind. They work closely with threat hunters to ensure that security measures are in place to detect and mitigate threats.

5. **Cybersecurity Consultant**: Experienced threat hunters may choose to work as independent consultants, offering their expertise to organizations that need help building or improving their threat-hunting strategies.

6. **Chief Information Security Officer (CISO)**: The CISO oversees the entire cybersecurity strategy for an organization, including threat hunting programs. This is a senior-level role requiring years of experience in threat detection, management, and overall cybersecurity leadership.

Real-World Example: A Day in the Life of a Threat Hunter in a Large Enterprise

In a large technology firm, **John Smith**, a senior threat hunter, starts his day by reviewing any alerts generated overnight by the SIEM system. These alerts may include unusual network traffic or failed login attempts. John immediately begins correlating these alerts with other data sources, such as firewall logs and endpoint data, to check for any signs of a potential attack.

After confirming that there is suspicious activity, he develops a hypothesis about the possible nature of the threat and starts gathering more data. This involves searching for any Indicators of Compromise (IOCs) such as unusual file access patterns or signs of malicious behavior on employee systems.

John works closely with the incident response team to escalate any verified threats, and together they implement containment measures to mitigate the risk of a breach. By the end of the day, John has written up his findings, updated the organization's threat intelligence platform, and shared his insights with the team to strengthen the company's defenses.

How to Start Threat Hunting as a Beginner

For beginners looking to break into the field of threat hunting, there are several steps to take that can help build a strong foundation and gain relevant experience.

Step-by-Step Guide to Becoming a Threat Hunter:

1. **Understand Basic Cybersecurity Concepts**: Before diving into threat hunting, it's important to have a solid understanding of basic cybersecurity concepts, such as types of cyber threats, attack vectors, and security tools. Start by taking online courses or earning certifications like **CompTIA Security+**.

2. **Learn Networking**: Threat hunters need to understand how networks operate. Take time to learn networking basics such as TCP/IP, DNS,

HTTP/HTTPS, and VPNs. Network administration certifications like **Cisco's CCNA** can be helpful.

3. **Familiarize Yourself with Security Tools**: Get hands-on experience with common cybersecurity tools such as SIEM, EDR, and network traffic analysis software. Many tools offer free trials or community versions that allow beginners to practice.

4. **Study Malware and Incident Response**: Threat hunters need to understand how malware works and how attacks unfold. Start learning about common types of malware (viruses, ransomware, worms) and how they infect systems. Gain knowledge about incident response protocols.

5. **Build a Lab Environment**: Set up a virtualized environment on your computer where you can practice threat hunting without risking real-world damage. You can simulate various attacks and practice your detection and response skills.

6. **Participate in Capture the Flag (CTF) Competitions**: Many cybersecurity enthusiasts participate in CTF challenges, which simulate real-world hacking scenarios and provide hands-on practice. These events help beginners hone their skills in a gamified environment.

7. **Network with Industry Professionals**: Join cybersecurity communities, attend conferences, and participate in online forums like Reddit's /r/ThreatHunting or LinkedIn groups. Networking will help you learn from others and stay updated on industry trends.

Real-World Example: A Beginner Threat Hunter's Journey in Securing a Network

Tom, a recent graduate with a degree in computer science, was passionate about cybersecurity but didn't know where to start. He began by taking a **CompTIA Security+** course and eventually earned his certification. Tom then got an internship at a small business where he assisted the IT team in monitoring network traffic and looking for suspicious activities.

After six months, he joined a **large cybersecurity firm** as a junior threat analyst. There, he worked under the guidance of senior threat hunters and gained hands-on experience using SIEM tools, analyzing logs, and correlating network data. With time, Tom became proficient in identifying potential threats and escalated a phishing attack that could have otherwise gone unnoticed.

This chapter explored how to build a career in threat hunting, from the essential skills and certifications to career pathways and practical tips for beginners. Here's a quick recap of the key takeaways:

- **Skills and Qualifications**: Threat hunters need a solid understanding of networking, operating systems, security tools, and data analysis. Certifications like CISSP, CEH, and GCTI can help boost credibility in the field.

- **Career Pathways**: Threat hunting is a specialized role within the broader cybersecurity field. Professionals can grow into roles such as security analysts, incident responders, or cybersecurity consultants, eventually reaching executive-level positions like CISO.

- **Getting Started as a Beginner**: Beginners should focus on gaining foundational cybersecurity knowledge, hands-on experience with security tools, and participate in CTF competitions to sharpen their skills.

Becoming a successful threat hunter takes time, dedication, and a commitment to continuous learning. By following the steps outlined in this chapter, you can start your journey in this rewarding and critical cybersecurity domain.

Chapter 14: Threat Hunting Challenges and Best Practices

Threat hunting is a vital part of cybersecurity, but it comes with its own set of challenges. Threat hunters are expected to be proactive, diligent, and adaptable as they seek out threats that might bypass traditional security measures. In this chapter, we'll explore the common challenges faced by threat hunters, the best practices for effective hunting, and how organizations can ensure their threat-hunting programs remain effective in the face of evolving threats.

Challenges Faced by Threat Hunters

While threat hunting is an exciting and rewarding job, it comes with several challenges. These challenges can hinder a threat hunter's ability to detect, investigate, and mitigate cyber threats efficiently. Below are some of the most common obstacles:

1. Resource Constraints

One of the biggest challenges faced by threat hunters is having limited resources. Security teams, especially in smaller organizations, often have to work with limited budgets, personnel, and tools. Without adequate resources, it becomes harder to dedicate the time and effort needed to thoroughly hunt for threats.

Real-World Example: Overcoming Resource Limitations

In a mid-sized retail company, a security team was understaffed but had to respond to a suspected breach. Despite being short-handed, the team leveraged **automation tools** and worked long hours, focusing on high-priority areas like endpoint monitoring and network traffic analysis. By identifying the specific compromised system early, they were able to contain the threat before it escalated into a full-scale attack. Their ability to triage and prioritize based on available resources played a crucial role in minimizing the impact of the attack.

2. Evolving Attack Techniques

Attackers are constantly evolving their tactics to bypass security measures. As cybercriminals develop new and more sophisticated techniques (e.g., advanced persistent threats, fileless malware), threat hunters must continuously adapt to stay ahead of these evolving threats. This means that threat hunters need to regularly update their knowledge and tools to identify the latest types of attacks.

3. Keeping Up with New Threats

With the rapid advancement of technology, new vulnerabilities, exploits, and threats appear on a regular basis. Threat hunters need to keep up-to-date with the latest threat intelligence, malware types, and attack vectors. This requires continuous learning and participation in industry forums, conferences, and threat intelligence sharing platforms.

Best Practices in Threat Hunting

Despite the challenges, threat hunters can follow best practices to improve their effectiveness and ensure that their efforts result in the early detection and containment of threats.

1. Build a Strong Foundation of Threat Intelligence

Threat intelligence is key to hunting effectively. Threat hunters need access to reliable threat intelligence feeds that provide information on the latest vulnerabilities, exploits, and attack tactics. By incorporating threat intelligence into their hunting strategies, hunters can make more informed decisions about where to focus their efforts.

2. Start with a Hypothesis

Effective threat hunting is driven by hypotheses. Instead of simply looking for "something wrong," threat hunters should craft a hypothesis based on available data or known attack vectors. For example, if an organization has recently been targeted by phishing attacks, the hypothesis could be that the attackers are likely to attempt lateral movement within the network. This allows hunters to focus their efforts on areas of greatest concern.

3. Leverage Automation and Machine Learning

Automation is a powerful tool for improving the efficiency of threat hunting. By automating repetitive tasks such as log analysis, data collection, and alert correlation, threat hunters can focus their attention on more complex aspects of the investigation. Machine learning and AI can also augment hunting efforts by identifying patterns and anomalies in large data sets.

4. Use a Layered Approach

Threat hunters should apply a layered approach to detecting threats, combining multiple data sources, such as endpoint data, network traffic, user behavior, and external threat intelligence. A multi-layered strategy ensures that even if one data source fails to identify a threat, others can step in to provide the necessary insights.

5. Focus on User and Entity Behavior Analytics (UEBA)

Threat hunting has increasingly shifted from focusing on signatures and known attack patterns to analyzing user and entity behavior. By establishing a baseline of normal user activity and network behavior, threat hunters can detect deviations that may indicate malicious activity, such as insider threats, account takeovers, or data exfiltration.

Real-World Example: Preventing a Major Breach

In a large financial institution, a security team implemented best practices to strengthen its threat-hunting program. They began by integrating **user behavior analytics (UBA)** into their monitoring systems, allowing them to flag unusual behavior (e.g., accessing sensitive data outside of normal hours). In one instance, UBA flagged an employee accessing customer data from an unfamiliar location, which turned out to be an attempt at data theft. By identifying this early, the team was able to prevent a major breach.

Continuous Improvement in Threat Hunting

The threat landscape is constantly changing, and the ability to adapt is crucial for threat hunters. To ensure that their threat-hunting efforts remain effective over time, organizations must focus on continuous improvement and evolve their hunting strategies. Here are some ways to do this:

1. Regularly Review and Update Hunting Techniques

As new attack techniques and tactics emerge, threat hunters should periodically review and update their hunting methods. This could involve learning new techniques, experimenting with new tools, or re-assessing the current threat-hunting hypotheses.

2. Conduct Post-Incident Reviews

After an attack or an incident, it's important to conduct a post-mortem analysis to identify what worked and what didn't. By reviewing past incidents and analyzing why certain threats went undetected, organizations can refine their detection strategies and improve their response procedures.

3. Share Knowledge Across Teams

Threat hunting should not operate in isolation. Collaboration between threat hunters, incident responders, and other security teams can improve overall security posture. Sharing knowledge and experiences about attack techniques, successful detections, and threat mitigation strategies can lead to better, more cohesive hunting efforts.

Real-World Example: Learning from Previous Attacks

In a multinational company, a threat-hunting team underwent a **post-incident analysis** after a sophisticated phishing attack. They realized that the phishing email bypassed their email filters because it used a novel tactic. The team immediately updated their email filters to account for this new method. They also introduced more thorough training for employees to recognize suspicious emails and phishing attempts. As a result, the company was able to prevent similar attacks in the future.

4. Invest in Ongoing Training and Tools

The world of cybersecurity is fast-paced, and threat hunters need to stay ahead of the curve. Investing in training, attending relevant conferences, and experimenting with new tools will help keep their skills sharp. Furthermore, organizations should ensure they have the right tools to support their hunting efforts, including automation platforms, machine learning models, and advanced analytics.

This chapter outlined the main challenges faced by threat hunters, including resource constraints, evolving attack techniques, and the need to stay current with new threats. It also highlighted best practices that can help threat hunters improve their effectiveness, including leveraging threat intelligence, starting with a hypothesis, and focusing on user behavior analytics.

Key takeaways include:

- **Challenges**: Limited resources, rapidly evolving attacks, and the need to stay updated with new threats.

- **Best Practices**: Build a strong threat intelligence foundation, start with a hypothesis, leverage automation and machine learning, and use a layered approach to threat hunting.

- **Continuous Improvement**: Regularly update hunting techniques, conduct post-incident reviews, share knowledge across teams, and invest in ongoing training.

Threat hunting is a dynamic, iterative process that requires continuous learning, collaboration, and adaptation. By following best practices and embracing a culture of continuous improvement, organizations can ensure they are prepared to detect and respond to threats as they evolve.

Chapter 15: The Future of Threat Hunting

As the cybersecurity landscape continues to evolve, so too does the field of threat hunting. With the increasing sophistication of cyber threats and the growing volume of data organizations must protect, the future of threat hunting looks promising but also increasingly complex. In this chapter, we will explore the role of automation, the shift towards predictive threat hunting, and the growing demand for skilled threat hunters. Each of these elements will play a significant role in shaping the future of threat hunting.

The Role of Automation in Threat Hunting

The growing complexity of cyber threats and the overwhelming amount of data that needs to be monitored and analyzed makes it increasingly difficult for threat hunters to manually detect every potential threat. As a result, automation is becoming a key player in modern threat hunting efforts.

How Automation Tools Like AI and Machine Learning Will Shape the Future of Threat Hunting

Automation can significantly enhance threat-hunting capabilities by reducing the burden of manual tasks and improving detection efficiency. Tools that leverage **Artificial Intelligence (AI)** and **Machine Learning (ML)** can sift through vast amounts of data quickly, flagging anomalies, identifying patterns, and even predicting future threats.

AI and ML are particularly useful in the following ways:

- **Automating repetitive tasks**: Automating log analysis, alert triage, and data collection allows threat hunters to focus on more strategic tasks.

- **Pattern recognition**: Machine learning algorithms can be trained to detect patterns of behavior that are indicative of malicious activity. These models become better over time as they process more data.

- **Reducing false positives**: By learning from previous incidents, AI tools can improve their accuracy, reducing the number of false positives that burden security teams.

Real-World Example: Streamlining Threat-Hunting Efforts with Automation

A large e-commerce company used **machine learning algorithms** integrated into their SIEM platform to monitor network traffic for unusual behavior. In one instance, the system flagged a series of unusual login attempts across multiple geolocations that human analysts might have missed. The automated system not only flagged the anomaly but also provided a recommended course of action. As a result, the company was able to block the potential attack before it escalated, reducing the time spent investigating and responding to the threat.

The Shift Towards Predictive Threat Hunting

Traditionally, threat hunting has been a reactive process, meaning that hunters respond to threats after they've been detected. However, with the increasing power of data analytics, there is a growing shift towards **predictive threat hunting**, where threat hunters leverage data to forecast and prevent potential attacks before they occur.

Moving from Reactive to Predictive Models Using Data Analytics

Predictive threat hunting involves the use of advanced **data analytics**, **machine learning**, and **threat intelligence** to predict where attacks are likely to occur and how they might unfold. By analyzing historical data, threat patterns, and emerging tactics, predictive models can identify potential vulnerabilities and forecast attack vectors.

Key advantages of predictive threat hunting include:

- **Early detection**: Predictive models can help spot early warning signs of an attack, often before the attack fully materializes.

- **Prevention**: By anticipating threats, organizations can take preemptive measures to block potential attacks before they even happen.

- **Better resource allocation**: By predicting likely attack targets, organizations can allocate resources more efficiently, focusing on the areas most likely to be attacked.

Real-World Example: Predicting and Preventing a Major Breach

A financial institution implemented a **predictive threat-hunting model** that analyzed behavioral patterns and external threat intelligence feeds to anticipate potential attacks. The system flagged a potential **insider threat** by identifying unusual behavior from an employee who had access to sensitive financial data. Using this predictive model, the institution was able to monitor the employee's actions in real-time, preventing a data breach that could have exposed millions of customers' financial information. This early intervention was possible due to predictive analytics that highlighted the employee's suspicious behavior before any harm was done.

The Growing Need for Threat Hunters

As the number and complexity of cyber threats continue to grow, the demand for skilled threat hunters has never been higher. Organizations are increasingly recognizing the importance of proactive security measures, and this is driving the need for specialized professionals who can track, detect, and mitigate sophisticated threats.

Increasing Demand for Skilled Threat Hunters

Several factors contribute to the increasing demand for threat hunters:

1. **The evolving threat landscape**: As new attack methods (such as ransomware, APTs, and fileless malware) emerge, there is a growing need for professionals who can anticipate and identify these threats.

2. **The rise in cybercrime**: Cybercriminals are becoming more organized and advanced, necessitating a dedicated workforce to combat these threats.

3. **The digital transformation of businesses**: As more businesses migrate to the cloud, adopt IoT devices, and implement digital transformation strategies, the attack surface grows. This creates new vulnerabilities and increases the need for threat hunters to secure these environments.

4. **Talent shortage**: Cybersecurity is one of the fastest-growing industries, but the supply of skilled professionals isn't keeping up with demand. There is a shortage of qualified cybersecurity workers, and this gap is particularly pronounced in specialized fields like threat hunting.

Real-World Example: Cybersecurity Talent Shortage

A global technology firm faced a significant talent shortage in their cybersecurity division. Despite having a robust security program, they struggled to keep up with the evolving threat landscape. To address this, they invested in upskilling their existing employees and partnering with universities to develop a pipeline of future cybersecurity talent. The firm also turned to **automation tools** to help manage the growing volume of alerts and data, allowing their smaller security team to focus on high-priority threats. However, the need for skilled threat hunters was still evident, as their reliance on automation could not replace the need for human expertise in complex threat detection.

The future of threat hunting is undeniably exciting, with new technologies and approaches continually reshaping the way threats are detected and mitigated. Key trends that will define the future of threat hunting include:

- **Automation and AI**: Automation tools powered by AI and machine learning will increasingly play a significant role in augmenting the capabilities of threat hunters, helping them analyze large data sets quickly and accurately, and improving the efficiency of threat detection.

- **Predictive threat hunting**: Moving beyond reactive methods, predictive models will enable organizations to anticipate and stop cyber threats before they materialize, providing an invaluable proactive approach to cybersecurity.

- **Increased demand for skilled professionals**: As cyber threats become more advanced and widespread, the need for qualified threat hunters will only grow. Organizations must invest in building and retaining skilled professionals to protect against an ever-expanding array of threats.

Threat hunters will remain a critical component of any cybersecurity strategy, but the tools and techniques they use will evolve rapidly. By embracing new technologies and staying ahead of emerging threats, organizations can ensure they are prepared for the future of cybersecurity.

Chapter 16: Threat Hunting Case Studies

In this chapter, we will explore real-world case studies that showcase the practical application of threat hunting. These case studies highlight how proactive threat detection, combined with advanced tools and methodologies, can prevent devastating attacks, safeguard sensitive data, and mitigate damage in various industries.

Case Study 1: How Threat Hunting Identified an Advanced Persistent Threat (APT) in a Financial Institution

Background:

A large financial institution had recently been targeted by an Advanced Persistent Threat (APT), a sophisticated and prolonged cyberattack aimed at stealing sensitive financial data. APTs are characterized by stealth, persistence, and careful planning, often going undetected for months or even years. In this case, the attackers used a combination of social engineering, spear-phishing, and lateral movement within the network to gain access to the institution's most valuable assets.

The Threat Hunting Process:

The financial institution had a robust security operations center (SOC) in place, but it was still relying heavily on traditional security tools such as firewalls and antivirus software, which often struggle to detect highly targeted APT attacks. To enhance their security posture, the SOC team implemented a **proactive threat hunting** approach.

- **Step 1: Hypothesis Creation**
  Based on threat intelligence feeds and unusual network activity, the security team developed a hypothesis that suggested an APT was active within the organization. The abnormal behavior, including connections to foreign IP addresses and unexpected outbound data traffic, provided initial clues.

- **Step 2: Data Collection and Analysis**
  The hunting team began gathering logs from various sources, including network traffic, endpoint data, and authentication logs. By analyzing the **domain name system (DNS) requests**, they identified that the system was making connections to known **malicious IP addresses**.

- **Step 3: Tracing the Attack Path**
  Using the **MITRE ATT&CK framework**, the threat hunters mapped the adversary's tactics, techniques, and procedures (TTPs). They identified the specific tools and methods the attackers used to move laterally within the network, including a **backdoor Trojan** used to escalate privileges and maintain persistence.

- **Step 4: Response and Mitigation**
  Once the attack was identified, the team immediately isolated the compromised systems,

blocked the malicious IP addresses, and began remediation efforts. The organization also conducted a full review of their network security policies to prevent future breaches.

Result:

The threat hunting team successfully identified the APT before it could cause any significant financial damage or compromise sensitive customer data. By detecting the attack early, the institution was able to implement containment strategies, significantly reducing the scope of the breach. The proactive approach saved millions of dollars in potential losses and reputational damage.

Key Takeaways:

- **Proactive detection** is key to identifying advanced threats like APTs before they cause significant harm.

- The **MITRE ATT&CK framework** is an invaluable tool for mapping and understanding the adversary's methods.

- **Threat intelligence** can play a crucial role in informing hypotheses and directing hunting efforts.

Case Study 2: Early Detection of a Ransomware Attack at a Healthcare Organization, Preventing Widespread Damage

Background:

A large healthcare organization with multiple clinics and hospitals across the country faced an imminent ransomware attack. The attackers used a **phishing campaign** to gain access to employee credentials, and the ransomware was designed to encrypt sensitive patient data. The healthcare industry is particularly vulnerable to ransomware, as the disruption of healthcare services can lead to significant operational, financial, and reputational consequences.

The Threat Hunting Process:

The organization's cybersecurity team, which was well-versed in threat hunting techniques, immediately began their search after observing unusual file access patterns.

- **Step 1: Hypothesis-Driven Approach**
  The threat hunting team, using threat intelligence on recent ransomware attacks targeting the healthcare sector, hypothesized that the phishing email campaign was just the initial phase of the ransomware deployment. They focused on **unusual file behavior** across the network, including large-scale file access and modifications, which are common during ransomware attacks.

- **Step 2: Data Collection**
  The team gathered data from multiple sources,

including **endpoint detection and response (EDR) tools**, **network traffic logs**, and **user access logs**. They identified that an employee's workstation had been infected with ransomware, which had begun encrypting files across the network.

- **Step 3: Detection and Early Containment**
  Through **behavioral analysis**, the threat hunting team noticed that the ransomware was trying to access multiple servers hosting patient data. They quickly alerted the system administrators, who isolated the affected systems, preventing the ransomware from spreading further.

- **Step 4: Incident Response and Mitigation**
  The incident response team worked closely with the threat hunters to identify the attack's scope and begin containment. They restored encrypted files from **backups**, ensured that all endpoints were secure, and implemented network segmentation to prevent future lateral movement.

Result:

By detecting the ransomware attack in its early stages, the healthcare organization was able to stop the encryption process before it could spread to critical systems containing patient data. The organization faced minimal operational downtime and did not need to pay the ransom. The rapid identification of the ransomware attack through threat hunting allowed for an effective incident response, ensuring the continuity of healthcare services.

Key Takeaways:

- Early detection is critical in mitigating the impact of ransomware attacks.

- **Behavioral analysis** and **data collection** across multiple layers (endpoint, network, and logs) can help spot ransomware before it causes widespread damage.

- **Collaboration** between threat hunters and incident responders is vital for quick containment and recovery.

Case Study 3: Insider Threat Detection Through Threat Hunting in a Retail Environment

Background:

A large retail chain experienced ongoing security incidents that involved **unauthorized access** to customer financial data. The company initially suspected an external attack, but after several failed attempts to trace the source of the data breaches, it became apparent that the issue could be an **insider threat**. Insider threats are particularly dangerous because they involve individuals who have legitimate access to the network and can bypass traditional security measures.

The Threat Hunting Process:

The retail company implemented a threat-hunting strategy aimed at detecting **insider threats** and uncovering any hidden malicious activity from within the organization.

- **Step 1: Hypothesis Creation and Data Collection**
  Based on employee access logs and known suspicious patterns, the team hypothesized that a disgruntled employee might be responsible for the data breaches. They started collecting detailed logs of employee activities, including login times, data access patterns, and file transfers.

- **Step 2: Behavioral Analysis**
  Using **anomaly detection algorithms**, the threat hunting team analyzed employee behavior to spot any deviations from typical activities. They identified an employee who had been accessing large amounts of customer financial data outside of their role's normal duties.

- **Step 3: Investigation and Confirmation**
  The hunting team conducted a deeper investigation into the suspicious employee's activity and uncovered evidence that the individual had been selling customer data on the dark web. The malicious activity was tracked across multiple endpoints, and the team found several **unusual file transfers** during off-hours, consistent with data exfiltration attempts.

- **Step 4: Containment and Response**
  The company quickly terminated the employee's access and began the process of alerting affected customers. They also worked with law enforcement to investigate the criminal activity. Following the breach, the organization implemented stricter access controls and more frequent audits of employee behavior.

Result:

Through proactive threat hunting, the retail company identified the insider threat before the employee could leak significant amounts of sensitive data. By acting swiftly, the company was able to minimize the damage, protect its customers, and maintain its reputation.

Key Takeaways:

- **Insider threats** can be as damaging as external attacks, and proactive threat hunting is essential for detecting and mitigating these risks.

- **Behavioral analysis** and **anomaly detection** are powerful tools for spotting insider threats.

- **Data exfiltration** should be a key focus for threat hunters, especially in organizations with sensitive customer data.

These case studies demonstrate the power of proactive threat hunting in identifying, mitigating, and responding to a wide range of cybersecurity threats. Whether dealing with advanced persistent threats, ransomware attacks, or insider threats, organizations that adopt a threat-hunting mindset can significantly reduce their exposure to cyber risks and ensure better protection of sensitive data. Through a combination of data collection, behavioral analysis, and collaboration between teams, threat hunting can be a crucial tool in maintaining a strong cybersecurity posture.

Chapter 17: Conclusion and Next Steps

As we wrap up this comprehensive guide to threat hunting, it is important to recognize that this field is far from static. The evolving nature of cyber threats, combined with advances in technology and the growing sophistication of attackers, means that threat hunting will continue to be a dynamic and essential part of cybersecurity.

The Ongoing Journey of Threat Hunting

Constant Evolution:

Threat hunting is not a one-time process; it is an ongoing journey. As new attack techniques emerge and cyber threats become more sophisticated, threat hunters must continuously refine their strategies, tools, and methods. The landscape of cybersecurity is constantly shifting, which means threat hunting practices must evolve in tandem to remain effective.

- **Adaptation to New Threats:** Attackers are constantly innovating, and threat hunters must stay ahead by adapting to these new tactics. For instance, ransomware attacks and APTs (advanced persistent threats) are continually changing, requiring threat hunters to develop new strategies to detect them.

- **Tools and Technology Advancements:** As machine learning and AI continue to advance, they will play an increasingly significant role in the automation and precision of threat hunting. Understanding how to integrate these technologies into your threat-hunting strategy is critical for the future.

Real-World Example:

A mid-sized company initially relied on basic security measures, such as firewalls and antivirus software, to detect and prevent attacks. However, after experiencing several targeted threats, the company invested in threat-hunting strategies, starting with manual log reviews and moving toward more automated processes. They developed a mature threat-hunting program, incorporating machine learning for anomaly detection and using the MITRE ATT&CK framework to map adversarial behaviors. This evolution allowed them to detect and respond to threats much more effectively, significantly reducing their exposure to cyber risks.

Resources for Continued Learning

The field of threat hunting is vast, and there is always more to learn. Whether you are just starting your journey or looking to deepen your expertise, there are numerous resources available to help you stay informed and develop new skills.

Books:

- **"The Threat Hunter's Handbook"** by **Steve Anson**
  A comprehensive guide that covers the methodology and tools used by threat hunters. It offers practical advice on setting up a threat-hunting program and includes real-world case studies.

- **"The Practice of Network Security Monitoring"** by **Richard Bejtlich**
  A classic in the field of network security, this book provides a deep dive into network traffic analysis, incident response, and how to detect and hunt for cyber threats in network environments.

- **"APT1: Exposing the China Cyber Espionage Group"** by **Mandiant**
  This book offers an in-depth analysis of one of the most well-known APT groups and provides insights into how they operate and how to detect and combat similar threats.

Courses and Certifications:

- **SANS Institute's Threat Hunting and Incident Response Course**
  SANS offers world-class training in threat hunting, incident response, and other critical aspects of cybersecurity. Their courses often include hands-on labs and real-world exercises.

- **Cybrary's Threat Hunting Course**
  Cybrary offers an accessible introduction to threat hunting, covering the basics and helping students develop practical skills they can use in their organizations.

- **Certified Threat Intelligence Analyst (CTIA)** by EC-Council
  This certification provides an understanding of how to analyze threat intelligence and apply it to a threat-hunting program. It's especially helpful for those wanting to build a more strategic, intelligence-driven approach to threat detection.

Online Platforms and Communities:

- **Krebs on Security** (https://krebsonsecurity.com)
  A leading blog by cybersecurity journalist Brian Krebs, offering in-depth insights into current threats, security trends, and cybercrime.

- **Reddit's /r/ThreatHunting**
  (https://www.reddit.com/r/ThreatHunting)
  A community of threat hunters where practitioners share experiences, techniques, and tools for hunting down threats. It's a great place for beginners and experienced professionals alike to learn from one another.

- **MITRE ATT&CK Framework**
  (https://attack.mitre.org)
  The MITRE ATT&CK framework is one of the most valuable resources for understanding adversarial tactics, techniques, and procedures (TTPs). It is continuously updated and offers practical insights into how to build your hunting strategies.

Real-World Example:

A cybersecurity professional with an interest in threat hunting started by taking an introductory course on

Cybrary. They then moved on to more advanced training with the SANS Institute and earned their Certified Threat Intelligence Analyst (CTIA) certification. With this foundation, they began applying threat-hunting techniques in their job, analyzing network traffic and logs to detect anomalous behavior. Their knowledge of tools like the MITRE ATT&CK framework allowed them to quickly identify and mitigate an attempted data breach, making them an invaluable member of their organization's security team.

Final Thoughts

Threat hunting is more than just a profession; it's a mindset. It requires curiosity, determination, and a constant willingness to learn. Every cyberattack that's thwarted, every piece of intelligence gathered, and every threat that is detected early contributes to a more secure digital landscape.

While the road to becoming an expert threat hunter may seem challenging, it is a journey that is well worth the effort. The rapidly growing field of threat hunting offers ample opportunities for those passionate about cybersecurity. Embrace the challenge, and remember that each hunt, whether successful or not, is a learning experience that contributes to your growth and expertise.

Motivation to Pursue Further Learning:

The demand for skilled threat hunters is higher than ever before. Organizations need individuals who can identify and neutralize threats before they cause harm. The skills you develop in threat hunting—ranging from data analysis and pattern recognition to advanced tools and techniques—are in high demand and can open doors to exciting career opportunities.

In this fast-paced, ever-changing field, your next step is to **continue learning**. Take advantage of the resources at your disposal, participate in communities, and never stop improving. Your contributions as a threat hunter will be essential in safeguarding the systems and data that businesses, governments, and individuals depend on.

Next Steps:

1. **Join Threat-Hunting Communities:** Engage in forums and online communities to learn from others and share your experiences.

2. **Practice and Apply Your Skills:** Set up your own lab environments to test and apply what you've learned.

3. **Pursue Advanced Certifications:** Look for advanced threat-hunting certifications and training programs that can help you specialize in the areas that interest you most.

4. **Stay Informed:** Follow blogs, attend webinars, and subscribe to security newsletters to stay up-to-date with the latest threats and tools.

By embracing the evolving nature of threat hunting, you will continue to grow in your role and contribute to the critical mission of securing the digital world.

www.ingramcontent.com/pod-product-compliance
Lightning Source LLC
La Vergne TN
LVHW022348060326
832902LV00022B/4316

* 9 7 9 8 3 0 1 3 0 7 6 8 3 *